BREAK IT NOW!

The Secret to Living in Freedom from Bad Habits, Negative Patterns and Addictions

BREAK IT NOW!

TD WILCOX

BREAK IT NOW! by TD Wilcox

Copyright © 2015-2016 by Tony D. Wilcox and Atomic Media Works, Inc.

No part of this book may be reproduced in any written, electronic, recording, or photocopying without written permission of the publisher or author. The exception would be in the case of brief quotations embodied in the critical articles or reviews and pages where permission is specifically granted by the publisher or author.

Although every precaution has been taken to verify the accuracy of the information contained herein, the author and publisher assume no responsibility for any errors or omissions. No liability is assumed for damages that may result from the use of information contained within.

All rights reserved, including the right to reproduce this book, or portions thereof, in any form.

Title ID: 5923608

ISBN-13: 978-0692596234

Cover Design: Atomic Media Works

Promotional website: **www.breakitnowbook.com**

Author's blog: **www.brokentobulletproof.com**

First Edition: December 2015

Printed in the United States of America

For my Fellow Strugglers...

you know who you are.

ACKNOWLEDGEMENTS

Special thanks goes out to my Bulletproof brothers; Mike, Tim, Mark, Jerry & Dan – I am forever grateful and indebted for your friendship. Thank you for watching my "SIX" at all times. This book could not have been written without you and your love for me. Special thank you to the staff and my ministry partners at Sandals Church in Riverside, CA - our "hospital" and place to be REAL with ourselves, God and others. To my daughters Tori, Abby, Mattea and Terra – you are beautiful lights in my world and gifts from the Lord. I am SO grateful for you all. To my wife, my love, my best friend Celeste – thank you for bravely walking this journey out with me in truth AND grace. Finally, to my Lord Jesus - the lover of my soul and truly the same yesterday, today and forever.

TABLE OF CONTENTS

INTRODUCTION
FREEDOM IS WITHIN REACH
BROKEN TO BULLETPROOF

PART ONE - "WHAT?"
THE SPECTRUM OF NEGATIVE BEHAVIORS
THE TRUTH OF NEGATIVE CONSEQUENCES
REPETITIVE BEHAVIOR IS NOT YOUR PROBLEM

PART TWO - "WHY?"
THE REASON EVERYTHING YOU'VE TRIED ISN'T WORKING
WHAT DOESN'T WORK
MASKS, ISOLATION AND SECRETS
ESSE QUAM VIDERI
THE WAY WE WERE MADE TO FUNCTION
WHO'S IN THE DRIVER'S SEAT
THE MISSING PIECE

PART THREE - "HOW?"
BREAK IT NOW AND LIVE IN FREEDOM
THE POWER OF COMMUNITY
THE POWER OF TRANSPARENCY
THE CORD OF THREE (OR SIX) STRANDS
WHO'S GOT YOUR SIX?
ACHIEVING PERFECTION (NOT)
STORIES
THE ACTION PLAN
LIVING IN FREEDOM

RESOURCES
THE AUTHOR

INTRODUCTION

FREEDOM IS WITHIN REACH

One of my favorite movie scenes of all is at the end of the movie Braveheart. Mel Gibson's character, the legendary Scot, William Wallace, is tied to a wooden cross and he is being publicly tortured and humiliated before his imminent death. The torture master directs a hooded torture administrator to carry out various acts of pain and dismemberment upon Wallace. With each act of pain inflicted, the torture master offers Wallace "mercy" if he'll just submit to the King. Wallace will not give his captors what they want - to BREAK him. The climax of the scene, and the movie for that matter, is when the torture master quiets that crowd and tells them that the prisoner wishes to speak. He fully expects Wallace to scream for "mercy" so they'll stop. Just before the torturer beheads him and ends his life, Wallace screams with everything he has left inside...not "mercy"...but instead..."FREEDOM!"

Isn't that really what we ALL desire so deeply? Freedom gives us the power to choose what is good for us and for others. Earlier in the movie, Wallace poses the question to the rag-tag band of Scots that had assembled to fight the wicked English King Longshanks, "What will you do without freedom?" This is a powerful question indeed - ESPECIALLY for someone who is held in bondage.

Thankfully, we don't suffer the bondage of a wicked King Longshanks in the physical world. But for those of us that have struggled or are struggling with negative patterns, bad habits or serious addictions, our captors can seem just as evil and depraved as Longshanks in a spiritual and emotional sense. They seem to sometimes have complete control over us or, at the very least, seem to be constantly pursuing us. Being under the control of a force greater than our own will is soul-crushing, regardless of how it manifests itself in our lives. These troubles come in many different forms, from annoying negative patterns like *not* paying the bills on time each month or biting your nails to more serious bad habits that produce a host of negative consequences like binge-eating, alcoholism, sex/pornography addiction or drug addiction. Regardless of what it is, these things can hold us in bondage and inflict serious emotional and spiritual pain suggestive of William Wallace's torture.

I should know. For most of my life, since I was in my late teens, I have struggled with addictive behaviors. Things that started as innocent curiosities gradually progressed over the years into serious, enslaving addictions in my life. I experienced a progression from drinking a few beers as a teenager, taking my first glance at pornography, using prescription medication for legitimate pain to full-blown problematic behaviors in my adult life THAT I COULDN'T STOP. By the time I was 47 years old, I found myself with a host of debilitating addictions that were causing major issues with my health, marriage, family, career, finances and relationships. I was no longer able to keep a lid on my secret behaviors. There really wasn't an area of my life that wasn't being affected negatively by my addictions. I needed help or I was going to die - THAT'S how bad it was.

Can you relate to any of that?

But the fact that you're reading this is proof that I didn't die! I've been able to progressively break the bondage of alcoholism, prescription drug addiction, pornography and sex addiction and a host of lesser bad habits and negative patterns in my life including biting my nails, a constant sense of striving and anxiety, tailgating others in my car and consistently paying the bills late. In a very real, but spiritual sense, I have been given the same FREEDOM that William Wallace was fighting for.

And that is why I've written this book. My life used to be centered around ME. I was an extremely self-centered, selfish person. Everything I did in my life was first and foremost designed to benefit ME, something pretty common with people that struggle with addiction. This resulted in a SLEW of negative consequences including a devastated marriage that was hanging by a thread, family turmoil, financial ruin, damage to my credit, damage to my career, damage to my reputation, a house in default, a car surrendered back to the bank, health problems, broken friendships - I could go on and on. Maybe you can relate to some of that as well?

Life is VERY different for me now. My marriage has been restored, my kids love and respect me, my career is blossoming, my finances are coming back into line, my credit has improved - life is GREAT and I have much to be grateful for. Now, instead of life being centered around benefitting ME, my life is focused on HELPING OTHERS. I work with men on a one-on-one basis and my wife and I work together with couples that struggle with difficult marriages, alcoholism, drug, porn and sex addictions and those just generally struggling with life and their spiritual well-being. I personally sponsor several men recovering from alcoholism and other addictions and I work with them weekly in their journey towards recovery and freedom. I speak to small and large groups and I have a passion for sharing my experience, strength and hope with others that *are struggling with negative patterns, bad habits or serious addictions like I did.*

I lived most of my life doing everything in my power to benefit one person – ME. I don't want to live that way anymore. I want to help others overcome the shame, frustration and negative consequences that come with these kinds of behaviors so they can finally achieve freedom. My hope is that this book will do that for YOU as well.

BREAK IT NOW is a treasure trove of information about recovery that I've learned in overcoming some serious substance and behavioral addictions in my life – an overview of the KEY things I've learned during my journey to freedom. These principles will help anyone held in the bondage of a negative pattern, bad habit or even a serious addiction. I've broken the book into three parts where we'll discuss…

- WHAT it is you're struggling with
- WHY you're having a hard time stopping on your own
- HOW you can achieve FREEDOM by doing something different

My goal is to open your eyes and heart to the things that allowed me to get well, experience recovery and redemption in my life and MOST importantly, how to find FREEDOM. Thank you in advance for trusting me with the privilege of helping another fellow struggler break free.

Blessings,

TD Wilcox
Author, Speaker and Addiction Recovery Mentor
Southern California

BROKEN TO BULLETPROOF

In order to put your own struggle into context and to help frame the concepts I'm going to lay out for you in this book, I'd like to share MY story with you so you can see the similarities between *your own* bad habits, negative patterns and addictions and the ones I struggled with. While the specifics and particularities of our struggles may be quite different, there is a common theme in bad habits, negative patterns and addiction that I want you to see because it holds the key to getting well which I'll reveal to you a bit later. As I briefly share my own experience, try to look for the similarities with how and what *you* are struggling with.

I had everything. No, really – I did. I had the American dream. I had the wife, the kids, the house, the cars, the job, the income, the friends, the health, the looks, college education, good reputation, success, respect. I HAD it.

And then one day I set off the grenade that blew it all to hell.

The problem was, it was all a lie. I had been living a lie for a long, long time. I had just walked out of a two-hour meeting with my wife. Her best friend and my best friend were also in attendance for emotional support. After 22 years of marriage, I had confessed to them that I had been living a secret life that included a long-term addiction to pornography which had led to unfaithfulness along with the serious abuse of alcohol and prescription drugs. I had outlined every sordid detail of my multiple addictions that I could remember since I was in high school. It was in a word brutal.

My wife was devastated. It was literally as if I had pulled the pin on a grenade and blown up all of our lives.

I was so ashamed of my secret addictions and behaviors that I couldn't bear to tell anyone. Over the years, there were brief instances when I had been partially truthful to my brother or to my roommates in college or maybe to a close friend or a pastor...but I was NEVER *completely transparent*. It was just *way too unbearable*. I had made a vow to myself that there were simply things I had done in my life that NO ONE would ever know; things I would take to the grave. It felt like if I told someone, anyone, what I had done...what I was STILL struggling with...I would die. The pain of shame was overwhelming and I had become a slave to it.

When I finally hit rock bottom and reached out for help, God was there. The voice of God can penetrate a heart regardless of circumstance. I know because my heart was filled with so much darkness, I thought I would never hear him again...*but I did.*

As I drove away from that meeting, headed back up to the mountains to the hotel room I was staying in, my wife sent me a text. It read this:

"I have never been more proud of you as a man than I am today. Thank you for having the courage to give me the truth."

While I knew I still had a very long, painful road ahead of me and I had no idea what it would look like (divorce was still a very real possibility), God had given me the courage I needed *to tell the truth, to be vulnerable, to be transparent.* It was the greatest leap of faith I had ever made in my life.

God showed up again a few hours later as I was driving the dark, winding mountain road back to the hotel where I was staying (I had been out of the house for several days). This time he would show up with words I desperately needed to hear. I was feeling like I had made a terrible mistake as I tried to navigate the mountain road through teary, swollen eyes. I knew I had now set in motion something that could not be reversed and I had no idea what it meant for my life going forward. I had an empty pit in my stomach and I was scared.

I knew I had crushed my wife's heart, shattered all her dreams and there was nothing I could do about it. I wanted to go get drunk so badly, but drinking was part of what had gotten me in this mess. I pounded on the steering wheel and tried to keep my SUV between the lines. What had I just done?

I cried out to God...

"Jesus! What will I do now? I just crushed my wife's heart! She is going to divorce me! I don't know how to live life without her! Without my kids! Please help me!"

Silence. Just the road noise of my vehicle, my breathing, my own pulse pounding in my head. I began to sob...again. My life had been reduced to a vale of tears.

I don't want to sound wacky and this is not an everyday occurrence for me, but I am familiar with "hearing" the voice of God. I've experienced him before, so I know what it's like when I'm in his presence. But this was different.

I heard what I can only call "the voice". It wasn't exactly audible, but at the same time it seemed as if it were inside the cabin of my SUV with me. It said...

"You are now like a clear sheet of glass."

"You are now like a clear sheet of glass."

A clear sheet of glass. My life had been so dark, so full of lies and deceit. I had been wearing a mask for most of my life, pretending to be someone and something I was not. It was as if my confession had wiped the slate clean. I understood that, but I didn't like it. I yelled back to the voice...

"I don't want to be a sheet of glass! Glass breaks and I don't want to break anymore!"

I pounded on the steering wheel and screamed it out loud and I meant it. I felt broken beyond repair and had no interest in ever experiencing that kind of pain again. I thought about drinking ...that would stop this pain.

The voice spoke again...

"As long as you keep telling the truth, you will be a clear sheet of BULLETPROOF GLASS."

"As long as you keep telling the truth, you will be a clear sheet of BULLETPROOF GLASS."

Bulletproof glass. That was good. I liked that. It was an unbreakable symbol I could hang on to. A symbol of strength and protection. It's transparent so that light shines through. Nothing is hidden, but all is safe behind bulletproof glass. It is like armor of light for my heart, my soul.

A verse came to mind... *"The night is nearly over; the day is almost here. So let us put aside the deeds of darkness and put on the armor of light." Romans 13:12*

Hope.

This imagery from God gave me hope in a desperate time of hopelessness. The thought that God would use my vulnerability to create a shield of transparent protection from the spiritual and emotional pain I was suffering gave me tremendous hope.

A new confidence rose up in my heart, a realization that my life was set on a new course now. Even though I had no idea where it would take me, this idea of living my life with transparency, authenticity...this was an exciting new proposition. Suddenly, long-forgotten verses from the Bible came flooding to mind with new meaning...

"To gain your life, you must lose it."

"My power is made perfect in your weakness."

I made the rest of the trip up the mountain with a hope-filled heart so grateful it overcame the fear that had engulfed me. I felt a shield around it that was impenetrable. That night, God met me in my very deepest despair and gave me a new heart, not of stone, but of flesh...and now protected by bulletproof glass. It was a new beginning with a new way to live life, a path away from the brokenness and heartbreak into a life of transparency, authenticity, a new-found freedom to be who God made me.

Here's what I can tell you about my experience. I used to be mastered by addictions and lived a duplicitous life to cover my actions. I lied perpetually, manipulated, deceived others, especially ones I loved and valued, in order to satisfy my own selfish desires. My marriage was on the brink of ruin. I lost everything financially. I compromised my health. I broke trust with almost everyone I cared for. I destroyed my reputation. I lost valuable friendships. I had legal troubles. Life was so dark for me that I reached a point where I contemplated death and even hoped for it. I can't imagine life being any darker.

Because I was willing to trust God enough to finally tell the truth, *I was set free*. Because I was willing to risk my heart by being completely vulnerable – to LOSE my life, I was GIVEN life back. Because I was willing to finally die to myself, my own strategies, my own striving and become WEAK, God showed his power in me. It is a fascinating exchange of opposites that God calls us into to experience his power and glory.

For me, this was the beginning of God's redemptive journey – from being completely BROKEN...to Bulletproof.

Can you see any similarities in your own story? If you're like most people that I meet who are struggling with bad habits, negative patterns and addictions, you probably can. In the next section, we'll unpack exactly what it is YOU are struggling with and take an honest look at the negative consequences associated with it.

BREAK POINTS:

- *If you stood before God today and He asked you what it was you are hiding from others that you are secretly ashamed of, what would it be?*
- *Name the one or more things that you secretly or openly struggle with and haven't been able to stop doing.*

PART ONE - "WHAT?"
WHAT IS YOUR BAD HABIT, NEGATIVE PATTERN OR ADDICTION?

What is it that is taking away, limiting or restricting your FREEDOM? In what ways do you find yourself LOSING CONTROL? It's a little different for everyone, but the act of *doing* something that you really don't want to do is something that is common to mankind, a problem that has been around for thousands of years.

Go back about 2000 years ago to the time of Christ. The most famous apostle of all – the most famous Christ- follower – was the apostle Paul. He is the man responsible for writing about a third of our modern day Bible. If *anyone* should have had this thing figured out, it should have been Paul. Yet we find him struggling with the very same thing as he laments in his letter to the Roman church…

"For what I am doing, I do not understand; for I am not practicing what I would like to do, but I am doing the very thing I hate."

- Romans 7:15

…and…

"For the good that I want, I do not do, but I practice the very evil that I do not want."

- Romans 7:19

That's EXACTLY how I felt in my own struggle with addiction. I felt like something else was controlling me. Why did I keep doing the things that I hated, that violated my own self-professed set of values? Most of the time, my addictions would kind of ebb and flow. Sometimes I'd feel like I was having victory over them...but other times I was completely enslaved and, all the while, telling no one.

On the *other* side of addiction, living a fully redeemed life of recovery, I've learned that LOTS of people I meet struggle in similar ways. Some struggle with drinking *too much* alcohol or drinking *too often* like I did. Some with marijuana or cigarettes or using prescription pills recreationally. Many men I meet struggle with viewing pornography or by acting out in illicit sexual activity. Some struggle with over-eating or simply making BAD food choices over and over. Some people can't stop less destructive bad habits like biting their nails, playing games on their phone, watching daytime soap-operas. Maybe it's the bad habit of constantly being late or rarely paying their bills on time. Regardless of how these things manifest themselves in people's lives, they are ALL frustrating, disappointing and some even dangerously risky or harmful behaviors and most of them come with lots of debilitating negative consequences. They are things we ALL want to stop or get control of...but we can't.

So what is YOUR negative pattern, bad habit or addiction that YOU are struggling with? Maybe you're struggling with MORE than one thing like I did. How BIG of a problem is it in your life? Is it causing some minor annoyances for you or producing some serious negative consequences? Is it a "socially acceptable" behavior that the rest of the world kind of "shrugs off" as simply normal or is it more shameful, something you do in private, a secret to be kept hidden? Are you struggling with a substance like alcohol, marijuana, prescription drugs, nicotine or caffeine? Or are you struggling with a behavior like biting your nails, cutting or compulsive eating?

My point is, just because these things come packaged in different forms, intensities and social acceptance levels, in an over-arching way they are ALL THE SAME in the fact that they *take away our freedom.*

These things take away our freedom.

These things have power over us and, at some point, we come to the frustrating realization that LIFE WAS NOT MEANT TO BE THIS WAY!

Indeed, it was NOT.

So in order to know what it is we need to be made free FROM...let's move forward and dissect exactly WHAT it is that you are struggling with.

NOTE TO READER: *It will be helpful for you to have a journal, notebook or notepad available. I will ask you at times to do some hand-written work as we move through the book and having a "Recovery Journal" or something of the sort will come in extremely handy.*

BREAK POINTS:

- *Create your own personal "recovery journal" to record your thoughts, ideas and progress.*
- *Write down specifically WHAT you hope to achieve by reading and working through the process outlined in "BREAK IT NOW".*

THE SPECTRUM OF NEGATIVE BEHAVIORS

Negative patterns, bad behaviors and addictions exist across a broad spectrum of intensity and seriousness. On the low-intensity and seriousness side we would place aggravating negative behavioral patterns like nail biting, consistently paying the bills late, frequently playing games on your phone to avoid stress, frequent social media consumption, etc. While these kinds of behaviors can be troublesome and put stress on relationships, they're not going to kill you. Just by their nature, they don't necessarily present a danger to the person or cause serious relationship damage when compared to other, stronger and more dangerous bad habits and addictions.

Negative Behavior Patterns – *these kinds of behaviors are aggravating, but not necessarily dangerous or posing serious harm to self or others.*

- Nail biting
- Nose picking
- Coffee, soda over use
- Sugar or fast food over use
- Frequent social media consumption
- Video games on phone, X-box, etc.
- Frequent or consistent late bill payment
- Unhealthy and frequent TV watching or movie attendance
- Gossiping
- Outbursts of anger, temper tantrums
- Swearing
- Chewing on the end of a pen or pencil

Bad Habits – *these kinds of habits can be more damaging and generate more serious negative consequences, health risks, damage to relationships, etc.*

- Erratic/aggressive driving that endangers others
- Road rage
- Smoking, chewing tobacco
- Binge eating
- Tattoos/piercing
- Unrestricted credit card spending

Serious Addictions – *these are much more serious behaviors that generate serious negative consequences and pose definite risks to personal welfare and relationships.*

- Alcoholism
- Prescription drug abuse
- Illegal drug use (heroin, cocaine, etc.)
- Marijuana use
- Over-eating
- Cutting or other forms of self-mutilation
- Pornography use
- Sex addiction

When it comes to the more intense addictions, they appear across a broad spectrum of intensity ranging from moderate to catastrophic. Below is a description of this spectrum including some of the typical characteristics of each range...

Addiction Intensity Spectrum:

- **Moderate** - Using more than 5 times per week, able to work and pay bills, loved ones questioning whether or not you are addicted, spending more than $100 a week on addiction
- **Severe** - Daily use is the rule, crashes, blackouts, withdrawal symptoms occur, difficulty in working, getting fired from jobs, using more than one substance (e.g., pot and alcohol), lying to loved ones and friends about use, loved ones urging you to get treatment, stealing from loved ones only to support addiction, cannot stop all use without help for longer than two weeks, suspended or revoked driver's license, arrested for possession or driving while impaired
- **Catastrophic** - Daily heavy use, cannot work to support self, stealing from loved ones, fighting with loved ones about use, stealing from strangers at least once, owing money to dealers, weight loss, liver problems, frequent sickness, cannot stop all use without help for longer than four days, spent up to 30 days in jail because of addiction, suspended or revoked professional license, family and friends are forcing you to get help
- **Terminal** - Daily heavy use; near continuous use, cannot stop all use without help for more than 24 hours, homeless or near homeless, regular stealing to support addiction, physical problems are getting worse, spent more than 30 days in jail because of addiction, have not been able to work at all, on probation for addiction-related offenses, you feel totally hopeless and unable to stop despite misery, friends and family have given up hope.

From: ***http://www.erptherapy.com/addictionintensityscale.asp***

It's important at this stage of our work to determine exactly what your struggle is and where do you fall in its seriousness. Part of getting well and moving into recovery is acknowledging exactly what your problem is. Are you dealing with a simple, less serious negative pattern, a bit more difficult-to-break bad habit or a full-blown addiction? Determine where you think you fall on the above spectrum and write it down. Be honest with yourself here, but regardless of where you fall on the scale, remember this: there is HOPE!

BREAK POINTS:

- *When was the LAST TIME you acted out your negative pattern, bad habit or addiction? Write down the specific DAY and DATE in your journal. This is your "sobriety date". You have just taken an important step in recovery! Congratulations!*
- *Write down how many days it has been from your "sobriety date" until today. If today is your sobriety date, that's OK! Write "DAY 1". Let's start counting the days that you are able to "make progress".*
- *Download a "SOBRIETY COUNTDOWN APP". We have several recommended free and paid apps available at our store website: www.brokentobulletproof.com/store or check the RESOURCES section at the end of the book.*

THE TRUTH OF NEGATIVE CONSEQUENCES

Every bad habit, negative pattern or addiction produces some sort of negative consequences. That's because these behaviors are counter-productive to the LIFE we are meant to fulfill, the life we were created for. Negative consequences are simply the natural product of God's perfect order. They are built into the system to point out when we are going off track.

Let me give you a few examples. Let's start with some mildly aggravating negative patterns many people fall into. We'll use the ones we've already mentioned, nail biting and not paying the bills on time. The negative consequences of nail biting would be things like pain or tenderness in the ends of your fingers, bleeding wounds that need to be bandaged, the social embarrassment of having others see that you bite your nails, etc. Having the bad habit of paying the bills late might produce negative consequences like being assessed late fees, damaging your credit, receiving embarrassing late notices in the mail, receiving annoying or embarrassing collection phone calls, etc. Because these negative patterns are fairly minor in the weight of their impact on your life, the negative consequences are usually minor as well.

More serious bad habits or addictions typically and eventually will bring more serious negative consequences. Consider bad habits like consistently speeding when you drive or frequent outbursts of anger at others. These kinds of bad habits will produce more painful consequences like, in the example of speeding costly speeding tickets, legal issues, time spent going to court, possibly damaging your own vehicle or the property of others, possibly experiencing personal injury in the event of an accident due to your speeding, etc. With the example of frequent angry outbursts, that might produce consequences like loss of valuable friendships, marital problems, disciplinary action at work or loss of a job, public embarrassment, etc.

Serious addictions like alcohol or drug abuse bring *even worse* consequences like DUIs, serious legal issues, jail time, loss of driving privileges, health problems like liver damage, pancreatitis or stomach and esophagus problems. A pornography or sex addiction can bring negative consequences like damaged intimate relationships, broken marriages, public humiliation, sexually transmitted diseases and more.

Part of breaking free from the bondage of these kinds of things includes TAKING RESPONSIBILITY for our actions. That means ACCEPTING whatever negative consequences our actions have produced. We can't get well if we fall into the trap of minimizing, excusing, ignoring or deflecting our responsibility for what we've done.

Therefore, it is helpful at this point to do the following:

1. Identify exactly WHAT you are struggling with – is it just ONE thing, or multiple? Is it a substance issue or a behavioral issue? Call it what it is and WRITE IT DOWN. This is an important step in acknowledging the problem or problems. "I have an addiction to _____" or "I struggle with the negative pattern of _____" or "I have a bad habit of _____".

2. Write down where you believe your struggle falls on the Spectrum of Behavior we discussed in the previous chapter. If you are struggling with a severe addiction, where do you think your

struggle falls on the Addiction Intensity Spectrum? Do you believe your struggle is MODERATE, SEVERE, CATASTROPHIC or TERMINAL?

3. List any negative consequences, minor or major, that you have experienced in the past or are currently experiencing due to your struggle. Be specific and detailed and write them ALL out. Write out every physical, financial, spiritual and emotional consequence that you can think of.

Grab your notebook, journal or a simple blank sheet of paper and a pen and HAND WRITE this exercise. Don't type it on a computer or tablet. The impact of our actions is best experienced as we watch the words flow out of the end of a pen or pencil held in our own hand. This helps us take ownership and responsibility for our consequences. Plus, this will become an important document to refer to LATER in your recovery so you can see the PROGRESS you've made from this point where you are starting. It is MOST helpful to do this work in your "recovery journal" or notebook so you can keep your work safe and organized in one place.

My point is, when we do things that go against God's natural order, compulsively or not, they ALWAYS bring some level of negative consequences. The GOOD news is, once we've broken these negative patterns, bad habits and addictions, the NEGATIVE CONSEQUENCES fade away or stop all together. THAT'S what we are going to work towards accomplishing in the coming sections.

BREAK POINTS:

- *Write down WHAT it is you are struggling with in a sentence that follows this format: "I have an addiction to _____" or "I struggle with the negative pattern of*

_____" or "I have a bad habit of _____".
(viewing pornography, taking pills, smoking marijuana, biting my nails, paying the bills late, etc.)

- *Determine how you would classify what you're struggling with as a negative pattern, bad habit or serious addiction, and write it down in your recovery journal.*
- *Where would you place your struggle on the "intensity spectrum of addiction" above? Make the determination and write it down in your journal.*
- *Write out every physical, financial, spiritual and emotional consequence that you can think of. You should be able to come up with at least 15 to 20!*

REPETITIVE BEHAVIOR IS NOT YOUR PROBLEM

I recently heard a man share his story of his alcohol addiction in a recovery meeting that I sometimes attend to help others struggling with addiction. He was celebrating two years of being clean and sober from alcohol. Here is what he said...

"I shouldn't even BE here right now. I should be in jail. Two years ago, I was scheduled to stand in front of the judge after I had been arrested for my Eighth D.U.I. I was facing a minimum of ten years in jail. While I was in my cell waiting for my court date, I finally surrendered. I got down on my knees and pleaded with God not to give me ten years. I told Him, if He would give me only three years in jail, I would never drink again. I would change my life. The next day, I stood in front of the judge and he asked me if I had anything to say before he handed down my sentence. I said, 'Your honor, if you send me back to jail, I won't get better. I have a serious problem. Just look at my record – I'm here for my Eighth D.U.I. I'm an alcoholic and I CAN'T STOP drinking. Putting me in jail isn't going to fix me. I need REAL HELP. I need a program that will show me how to get better. I know if you put me in jail, as soon as I get out, I'll start running with my old crowd and I'll drink again if I don't get some real help. That's all I have to say.'

The judge called for a recess and he took my attorney and the prosecuting attorney back into his chambers. They were back there for over an hour. When they finally came out, the judge asked me to stand up and he says, 'Your story touched me. I believe you really do need some help and I think you're right about going back to jail. That's why I'm not going to send you there. I'm going to let you go home with the agreement that you will go to Alcoholics Anonymous and get help.' So that's why I'm here today. I should be in jail right now, but I did what the judge told me to do and now I don't have to drink anymore. Alcoholics Anonymous helped me realize that drinking alcohol wasn't my real problem, it was just a symptom. My real problem was much deeper than that. My real problem was ME! A.A. helped me figure out how to deal with the real problem and gave me my life back."

Eight D.U.I.s! This man admitted *he couldn't stop drinking.* He experienced the negative consequences of eight D.U.I.s, a lost job, a lost driver's license, canceled insurance, legal bills and was facing ten years in jail…and NONE of that was going to keep him from drinking again. He admitted to himself that alcohol was NOT his problem.

This is the case with most of these negative patterns, bad habits and addictions that we've been talking about. The addiction itself, the repetitive behavior, even the dependency on a substance is NOT the real problem. Nail biting, paying bills late, popping pills, looking at porn, smoking marijuana, compulsive overeating, cutting – NONE of these things are the *real problem*. Just like the man said, the REAL problem goes MUCH deeper.

Did you notice what the man said the REAL problem was? He said "The REAL problem was ME!" He's EXACTLY RIGHT. Let me explain what the man is talking about.

Here is what the cycle of addiction looks like:

EMOTIONAL TRIGGER: *We experience feelings of incompetence, insignificance or impotence.*

CRAVING: *These feelings bring emotional/spiritual discomfort, causing us to crave RELIEF.*

PRE-OCCUPATION: *Our minds start working overtime to create a strategy to relieve or satisfy the craving.*

ACTING OUT: *We engage in the chosen, usual negative behavior, bad habit or substance intake in order to satisfy the craving.*

GUILT/REMORSE: *We experience guilt and remorse which leads to MORE feelings of incompetence, insignificance or impotence and the cycle starts all over again.*

I'm not aware of ANY negative pattern, bad habit or addiction that doesn't follow this model in almost every way. In this model, the BEHAVIOR or SUBSTANCE is not the driving force. The driving force is INTERNAL and has to do with the EMOTIONAL and SPIRITUAL forces brought on by THE WAY WE THINK ABOUT OURSELVES. THIS is what is at the root of addiction. This is why that man said, "the real problem is ME!"

What does it mean to feel *incompetent*? The dictionary definition is *"not having or showing the necessary skills to do something successfully"*.

How about *insignificant*? *"Too small or unimportant to be worth consideration"*.

Impotent? *"Unable to take effective action. Helpless, powerless."* The BEGINNING of the cycle of addiction is when we start thinking things about ourselves like:

"I'm not good enough" or "I'm not strong enough."

"Nobody cares about me."

"I can't do anything right."

"I suck."

ALL of this kind of negative self-talk gets "summarized" in our minds so that we form one, cohesive negative opinion of ourselves which typically sounds like…

"I'm no good."

Who wants to feel like THAT? Look, here's the problem. When we walk around for very long telling ourselves that we're NO GOOD and maybe our situations or relationships seem to validate that idea, sooner or later, these things become more than just some negative thoughts – they become our IDENTITY. *We start believing our own lies about ourselves!*

This is a very subtle process and you'll have to look deeply into your own heart to find how you're hearing this kind of self-talk.

The Big Book of Alcoholics Anonymous, the undisputed authority on the 12 steps and addiction recovery, says this about the root cause of addiction:

> *"Selfishness - self-centeredness! That, we think, is the root of our troubles. Driven by a hundred forms of fear, self-delusion, self-seeking, and self-pity, we step on the toes of our fellows and they retaliate. Sometimes they hurt us, seemingly without provocation, but we invariably find that at some time in the past we have made decisions based on self which later placed us in a position to be hurt.*
>
> *So our troubles, we think, are basically of our own making. They arise out of ourselves, and the alcoholic is an extreme example of self-will run riot, though he usually doesn't think so."*
>
> *- Alcoholics Anonymous, pg 62*

Being selfish and self-centered doesn't mean we think too highly of ourselves. It means we think TOO OFTEN of ourselves. If we are thinking *too often* that we are BAD, that is a type of spiritual and emotional pain that DEMANDS relief. The reason this kind of thinking is so uncomfortable is because it is in direct conflict with our true selves – the way God REALLY sees us. We are VALUABLE to Him and for us to think differently brings about an uncomfortable, internal spiritual tension that is almost impossible to withstand.

You are not alone. The fact is that with most people in the world, relief comes through some type of negative pattern, bad habit or addiction. It might SEEM like the addiction is the problem, but it's not. If it was, you'd just STOP doing what you are doing, right? There is something deeper driving the behavior and in the next section, I'll discuss WHY this is the case.

BREAK *POINTS:*

- *Write down the common "emotional triggers" that cause you to experience feelings of incompetence, insignificance and impotence.*
- *Think back to the last time you experienced one of these triggers. Can you remember what the "self-talk" sounded like at this time? Write down the negative things you said to yourself. Be BRUTALLY honest. This exercise is important to help you develop a strong sense of "self-awareness" as we move forward.*

PART TWO – "WHY?"

THE REASON EVERYTHING YOU'VE TRIED ISN'T WORKING

In mid-2010, I was asked by a friend to join his cycling team that was going to participate in the 2011 Race Across America. I wouldn't call myself an "avid" cyclist at the time by any means. I owned a bike, but that was about it. "You want me to ride my bike across the country with you?" I asked, slightly dumbfounded. "Yes," he replied.

I LAUGHED at him. Literally. To me, this was simply a hilarious proposition. Probably the most I had ever ridden my bike at one time was about 10 or 12 miles and I had almost died when I did that. He brushed off my insulting laugh and just said, "Pray about it."

I was definitely experiencing some negative consequences from my drinking and other addictions at the time. My marriage was struggling, I was just coming off about a year long stint of taking narcotics for a serious neck surgery I had in 2009, I was drinking as much as I could without completely letting it get out of hand and I was hiding a lot of it as well. I did pray about it and after a few weeks I decided maybe training for a monumental bike race would be just the thing I needed to get my life back on course. I called up my friend and told him I was in. I also made a vow to STOP drinking all alcohol until after the race was over. I knew I couldn't train for the race and keep drinking. The training was going to be intense as we worked ourselves up to riding over 100 miles a week before the actual race and had included several 70 to 110 mile rides at a time. In the back of my mind I thought, if I can stop drinking for nine months while I train, by the end of the race I should be cured. Right?

WRONG.

I did stop drinking for those 9 months. At least I stopped putting alcohol in my system. But I didn't stop THINKING about it. That's no way to live life. I was amazed by how often I THOUGHT about drinking when I wasn't drinking. This is called "white-knuckling" sobriety. I was what is commonly referred to as a "dry" drunk. I trained for the race, got in great shape and finished the Race Across America with my 8-man team without taking a drink. It was a great accomplishment, one of the real highlights of my life. Yet I was still miserable. The problem was, I was treating the SYMPTOM and not the actual problem – my own self-centeredness and selfishness.

In this section, I'm going to discuss WHY the typical, well-intentioned strategies most people take to break negative patterns, bad habits and addictions just don't work. Then we'll be able to work on the REAL problem.

WHAT DOESN'T WORK

I like to refer to the Big Book of Alcoholics Anonymous often because it is the definitive standard for addiction recovery with its proven 12 Step method of recovery. There's a great section in the book of Alcoholics Anonymous that talks about all of the self-imposed restrictions that alcoholics try in order to stop drinking *that don't work.* Here's part of it...

"Here are some of the methods we have tried: Drinking beer only, limiting the number of drinks, never drinking alone, never drinking in the morning, drinking only at home, never having it in the house, never drinking during business hours, drinking only at parties, switching from scotch to brandy, drinking only natural wines, agreeing to resign if ever drunk on the job, taking a trip, not taking a trip, swearing off forever (with and without a solemn oath), taking more physical exercise, reading inspirational books, going to health farms and sanitariums, accepting voluntary commitment to asylums—we could increase the list ad infinitum."

- Alcoholics Anonymous, page 32

The point is, those of us struggling to stop negative patterns, bad habits and addictions - even serious ones like alcoholism, will go to all sorts of lengths and try all kinds of methods and strategies to help us STOP the bad behavior. Some of them will have an impact some of the time, but rarely do these kinds of self-imposed strategies do anything other than set us up for another disappointing failure, further setting in place the cycle of addiction.

Let's go back to our minor negative patterns we've used as examples - nail biting and frequently paying the bills late. One self-imposed strategy to help break a nail biting pattern that was used on me as a kid (my mom actually tried this on me because I couldn't stop biting my nails as a teenager) is to put hot sauce like Tabasco® on your fingertips. The idea is to use a negative-reinforcement to stop the behavior. It didn't work. I started actually developing an appreciation for the flavor of Tabasco® and I use it often today!

Another strategy I've seen people use to help get the bills paid on time might be online services like bill-pay or a calendar reminder system. Maybe they help, maybe they don't. The problem with all of these kinds of efforts is that they miss dealing with the real root of what's driving the negative behavior – the way we are THINKING about ourselves. The more we pay the bills late, the more negative consequences pile up and the more we start thinking things like, "Wow. I SUCK at managing my finances."

When I first started trying to deal with my own struggle with pornography, one of the things I did was to put accountability software on my computers. This was helpful to a degree in that it helped me to start the process of thinking differently about what I was viewing on the computer and knowing I would have to answer to someone about it, but it still didn't solve the root problem – the way I thought about myself when I experienced the feelings of incompetence, insignificance and impotence. Adding a filter or piece of software on my computer wouldn't help me with how I was processing emotion and the ways I strategized to resolve what I was feeling.

Don't get me wrong – there is a perfect need for things like pornography filters, online bill-pay software and other pre-emptive measures like this (maybe even Tabasco® sauce!), especially at the beginning of recovery when things are foggy and emotions are hard to get a grip on. The merry-go-round needs to slow down for us to get off. Folks recovering from serious addictions need structure because life has been so chaotic so anything that can bring clarity and structure is helpful in recovery. BUT…the truth is that these kinds of things like porn filters, solemn vows, commitments to go to "90 meetings in 90 days" and such need to be recognized for what they are – helpful and even necessary tools in getting better – but they are NOT in and of themselves the solution. The solution comes from acknowledging the root of the problem, treating the actual disease and not just the symptoms. But before we get to the solution, I want you to realize what your coping strategy probably looks like if you are anything like I was. I coped by HIDING what was really going on. Check out my strategy of hiding, lying and mask wearing in the next section - maybe you can relate?

BREAK POINTS:

- *Write down all of the ways you've tried to manage and "white knuckle" your negative pattern, bad habit or addiction on your own.*
- *Can you relate to hiding your behavior or "wearing a mask"? If so, explain how and write it out in your journal.*

MASKS, ISOLATION AND SECRETS

One of the things that impedes the process of breaking the cycle of addiction is the system of strategies we create to accommodate our struggle. These typically come in the form of mask-wearing, isolation and the keeping of secrets from others which usually include lies, deception and manipulation. These are all strategies for hiding behaviors and they, like our bad habits, negative patterns and addictions, occur across a spectrum of seriousness and intensity. I became a master at ALL of these methods when I was in the grips of my own addictions. Let me explain.

A mask is a covering for all or part of the face, worn as a disguise. When worn effectively, a mask hides the true self and leads others to believe that you are in fact someone other than who you really are. Everyone wears a mask in some form or another and for different reasons. For me, I wore a social, spiritual and emotional mask to hide my secret life. I wore a mask because I wanted to be accepted by my friends, my wife, my children, my co-workers, etc.

Most people struggling to break a negative pattern, bad habit or addiction wear a mask in one form or another because they are **ashamed** to let people see them for who they truly are or to let others know what's really going on. People mostly wear masks because of **shame**. Best-selling author and shame researcher Brene' Brown defines shame as "the fear of disconnection."

SHAME is the "fear of disconnection".

Shame says, "You're not good enough. If others knew who you REALLY are, they would reject you." This is why I wore my mask and hid my secret behaviors - because of *shame*. Regardless of how nice I made it look on the outside, how smart, articulate, funny or talented I made others think I was...inside I was dying, trying to find ways to alleviate the feelings of incompetence, insignificance and impotence that I was experiencing. I believed that if others really knew me, they would hate me. If they really knew the things I had done, the ways in which I had tried to fulfill my secret desires that I couldn't control, they'd be repulsed and I'd be rejected. I believed this lie to the core of my being. I believed it of my friends, my boss, my pastors, my extended family, my kids and my wife. I was FULLY committed to wearing the mask. I HAD to wear the mask. It was a matter of life and death for me. If I took off my mask, I BELIEVED I would die, so I became a master of keeping it in place.

Masks can come in the form of emotional or physical manipulation. I might keep a mask in place that projects a persona that "I've got it all together" by not letting my anger get out of hand when inside I'm secretly seething or through false humility or by saying polite things I don't mean. I might use physical apparatuses to project a persona to others like the kind of car I drive or the kind of watch I wear – if you think I'm super-successful, you couldn't imagine me struggling with a secret bad habit or addiction, right? Nail biters (ladies at least) may try to hide their nails with acrylics applied on top to cover the damage. Cutters may hide scars under clothing. These are all really just forms of mask wearing – creating an outward appearance that is different from reality.

Another strategy that gets in the way of breaking these behaviors is isolation, especially in the case of those struggling with more serious addictions. If others can't see what we're doing, we don't have to worry about them nagging us about it or we don't have to worry about being ashamed by our behavior. Isolation is achieved simply by spending time alone. For the porn addict, it's waking up in the middle of the night when everyone else is asleep so they can secretly view pornography. For the alcoholic it might mean drinking in secret, hiding bottles of alcohol strategically around the house or at work so they can take a secret swig unnoticed. For the sex addict, it's sneaking away to seedy hotel rooms. Nail biters might lock themselves in a bathroom stall or hide behind a computer screen to bite their nails. The less they have to be around other people that *really care* about them or *really know* them, the less chance they have of being exposed. Isolation limits the opportunity for others to give us the help we really need to break these strongholds.

Probably the most common strategy to hide behavior is the keeping of secrets. No one *wants* others to know about embarrassing behaviors, patterns, habits or addictions that can't be broken. That's only natural. That's why it's so easy to develop the strategy of keeping these behaviors hidden. Keeping secrets simply means I *don't* tell others that I'm having a hard time keeping a behavior under control. It's being *inauthentic* with others. When I was in the throes of my alcohol addiction, I would tell my wife or others that, "I only had a few beers." That was a partial truth – yes, I had three beers that *they* saw me drink. They didn't see the two or three shots of tequila I put on top of the beer that was in the small airline bottles I had hidden in my back pocket or socks and downed in the bathroom when no one was looking. Secrets come in the form of denial also – "I don't struggle with looking at pornography. That's disgusting." Or in the form of outright lies – "I haven't taken a pill in over 30 days. Really." I've used ALL of these strategies in order to hide my own shameful behaviors.

Here's one of the biggest problems with wearing a mask, isolation and secrets: **when we don't express our true selves and show real feelings, we are prevented from experiencing real intimacy in relationships.** These strategies simply won't allow us to develop deep, meaningful relationships because they are all built on a false perception. Not only does it hinder the development of trust in our relationships, but we aren't *being* who we really are - our TRUE selves - which is what I want to discuss next.

BREAK POINTS:

- *How would you describe the type of mask you wear? For example, the "I've got it all together mask" or the "you should be afraid of me because I'm a tough guy" mask. Be descriptive and write it in your journal.*
- *What other strategies have you used to hide your negative pattern, bad habit or addiction? Be specific and write them all down.*

ESSE QUAM VIDERI

Constantly propping up a persona with mask wearing, isolation and secrets is exhausting and depressing. It takes a lot of energy, strategizing and manipulating to keep a mask in place. For me, this process was so exhausting that it fed my need to medicate *even more*. It also developed in me a serious sense of anxiety, fear and paranoia – I could be exposed and found out at any moment. Add to all this exhaustion, anxiety, fear and paranoia the steady pressure of knowing deep inside that I was really just a fraud, a poser… and at some point it just becomes unbearable. This is an awful, crushing and debilitating way to live. It literally sucks the life out of a soul. Regardless of the motivation, almost everyone on earth is pretending to be someone other than who they actually are.

I have a sign in my office with a simple phrase in Latin; "Esse quam videri". It means *"To be, rather than to appear."*

Esse quam videri - "to be, rather than to appear"

I'm not a tattoo guy, but *if I was,* I would have this phrase etched on a cross – to me that would be a cool tattoo. I think it resonates so deeply with me now that I've recovered from such serious negative patterns, bad habits and addictions because I have a proclivity to live exactly in the opposite manner of this phrase. My phrase would have been the opposite: "Videri potius quam" - *"to appear, rather than to be".*

For most of my life, when I interacted with other people, I found myself *working* to manipulate *what they thought of me.* It was almost impossible for me to just "be myself" around others. I constantly had my radar on high alert, trying to gauge what others thought of me in order to get a sense of personal satisfaction in myself. My sense of "being OK" came from what my wife, my family, my parents, my boss, my employees - almost ANYONE - thought of me. That meant that I ALWAYS had to be presenting a polished, perfect version of myself and I was powerless to just BE REAL in the presence of others. It was truly exhausting.

Here is where I'm going with all of this; since the root of these negative patterns, bad habits and addictions comes from self-centeredness and selfishness - the way we THINK about ourselves and the amount of time we spend doing it - we live NOT wanting others to see that in us. We don't want people seeing us for who we really are – whether that be a person that bites their nails, pays their bills late or has bad credit to someone with a serious pornography, alcohol or drug addiction. Across the spectrum of negative behaviors, NONE of this is stuff we want out in the open. It's all dirty laundry, right? The *shame* of these behaviors is what keeps us bound in the cycle of negative behaviors and addiction. We live, at least in matters of these behaviors, in isolation and with underlying emotions covered by masks and secrets allowing us to present to the world a persona that is *false.*

The presentation of this false self only perpetuates our self-centered, selfish life and further fuels our bad behavior...with the WRONG kind of fuel, which is what I'll discuss in the next section.

BREAK POINTS:

- *Describe what you think it would look and feel like to present your "true self" to the world and those around you. Write this down in your journal.*
- *Draw a line down the center of a journal page. On the left, write the title "How I think others view me" and on the right, write the title "How I view myself". Write out a detailed description under each heading and compare the two. BE BRUTALLY HONEST with yourself!*

THE WAY WE WERE MADE TO FUNCTION

I want to use an engine metaphor to make the following point. A diesel engine is a highly sophisticated piece of machinery, built more stoutly than a typical gas engine so it can handle the high compression rates that are produced when diesel fuel burns. Diesel fuel is different than gas. It's much heavier and denser than regular gasoline. Diesel engines also differ from gasoline engines in that they don't use a spark plug. They create a tremendous amount of horsepower and torque – that's why they are so effective at pulling heavy loads. Because a diesel engine is specifically created to burn only diesel fuel, *bad things happen if you put a different kind of fuel in it.* Here's what one website says will happen if you put *regular* gasoline in a diesel engine:

> *Gasoline is formulated to resist auto-ignition in a spark engine, so this fuel introduced into a diesel engine either won't ignite or will (much more likely) ignite at the wrong time causing severe detonation. Though diesel engine reciprocating components (pistons, wrist pins and connecting rods) are built to withstand enormous explosive force, the shock wave effects of uncontrolled detonation can easily destroy them.*
>
> *In addition to the specific burn characteristics that diesel fuel and biodiesel afford to compression ignition diesel engines, the fuel itself acts as a lubricant for the fuel pump and delivery system as well as the valve train (recall that diesel fuel is actually a very light oil). Running thin, low viscosity*

gasoline through a diesel fuel system would starve it for lubrication and cause those sensitive components to rub together (metal-to-metal) eventually destroying them.

http://alternativefuels.about.com/od/dieselbiodieselvehicles/a/gasolinindiesel.htm

Here's the point: put the wrong kind of fuel in a diesel engine and it will destroy it. Human beings are exactly the same.

Put the wrong kind of fuel in a diesel engine and it will destroy it. Human beings are exactly the same.

We were also specifically designed to run on a very specific type of fuel: *relationship with God.*

All of us, from our very first breath have a need for God. Think about this: we had NO PART in our own creation. We weren't asked for our opinion or choice in the matter, we were just "born". From our very first breath we were *in need* of something we could not generate on our own or provide for ourselves. In the Bible, Jesus describes this need in every person as a "thirst"...

"Those who drink of the water that I will give them will never again be thirsty. The water that I will give will become in them a spring of water gushing up to eternal life." John 4:14

Of course he is speaking in spiritual terms. He is talking about a thirst in our hearts, a thirst that ONLY A RELATIONSHIP WITH GOD CAN SATISFY. But here's our problem – we *insist* on trying anything and everything *other* than God as the fuel to power our lives. We insist on turning to all kinds of other things in this world to meet our spiritual thirst.

In my own life, I tried countless things to fill the aching hole in my heart – the "God" hole that only He can fill. I tried alcohol, pills, porn, sex, food, music, success, money, recognition, nice cars, a big house, nice clothes - I could go on and on.

News flash: NONE OF IT WORKS.

It's just like putting gasoline into a diesel engine. It "feels" like its working, but in reality it is destroying us on the inside. The truth is we really can't accomplish much of anything that is spiritually good or valuable apart from God. Jesus told us this also...

"I am the vine; you are the branches. If you remain in me and I in you, you will bear much fruit; apart from me you can do nothing." John 15:5

If I am apart from God, I'm left with just "me" to run my life and that's a COMPLETE TRAIN WRECK. I tried that. I was a *horrible* CEO of my own life. My very best thinking, strategizing, trying of alternative fuels, etc. landed me passed out, face down on the asphalt in a pool of blood, into jail and then into rehab. Nice.

Here's the reality; I can't generate my *positive spiritual condition*, my own love, joy, peace, patience, kindness, goodness, faithfulness, gentleness or self-control *at any sustainable level* on my own. I MUST have God for those things because these things are positive "spiritual" forces. And those are the very things I sought when I was caught in the addictive cycle and experiencing feelings of *insignificance, incompetence and impotence* - which are fueled by negative "spiritual" forces like fear, resentment, doubt and worry. When I felt those things, what I really needed was peace, love and joy and those are spiritual forces that come from God in abundance. I tried to find them in a bottle or a pill or through a host of other things that just kept leaving me feeling empty. I had to hit my own personal rock bottom to understand fully, once for all, that I was created to run on a different kind of fuel, fuel I could ONLY get from one place.

BREAK POINTS:

- *What kinds of things have you used as "fuel" to power your own life? Write these things down in your journal.*
- *Have you ever had a time when you've experienced God as the "fuel" of your life? If so, describe that experience and write it down also.*

WHO'S IN THE DRIVER'S SEAT?

I get it. No one wants to admit to selfish or self-centered behavior. It's ugly at its core and no one would want to be identified as "selfish". I didn't either. But it wasn't until I really took a hard, honest look at my TRUE motives for even my smallest, most insignificant actions that I began to see that I operated from a position of selfishness in almost every way and that *this was at the root of almost every negative behavior in my life*. Totally depressing.

We've established that we were created to run on the fuel of God in our lives. Things happen to us every day that cause us to feel the feelings of insignificance, incompetence and impotence in our lives. We're late for work and the boss yells at us or gives us the eye and we feel incompetent. We get a bill in the mail that we can't pay and we feel impotent. We get ignored or dismissed by a friend or colleague and we feel insignificant. These are normal, everyday occurrences. It's what we do with these feelings that determines if we will fall into negative behavioral patterns, bad habits or develop addictions. What we do with these feelings comes down to WHO IS IN THE DRIVER'S SEAT of our lives.

Here's what I mean. Let's face it – these feelings are uncomfortable. It is totally natural to want to be out of the discomfort of feeling insignificant, incompetent or impotent. Sitting in those feelings without acting out or medicating the discomfort in an attempt to take the power out of these feelings is hard spiritual work that takes real discipline...*or an effective alternative plan.*

What MOST people do with these feelings is that we strategize to determine what is the fastest, most effective method to stop the discomfort that has the potential for the least amount of negative consequences.

> *...we strategize to determine what is the fastest, most effective method to stop the discomfort that has the potential for the least amount of negative consequences.*

We utilize whatever substance or behavior that is within our sphere of power. It could mean drinking a few beers or taking a shot of liquor, smoking a joint, taking a pill, taking a nap, eating a sugary treat, looking at porn, masturbating, having sex, biting our nails, zoning out on a video game or movie, smoking a cigarette. ALL of these things WORK to one degree or another in alleviating the discomfort. And because they work, they easily turn into habits, patterns and addictions that are enslaving to one degree or another across the behavior spectrum. WE WERE NOT DESIGNED TO LIVE THAT WAY! And here's the interesting thing about all of these things (and a thousand others like them); they all are done primarily to satisfy SELF. Most of them don't take any interaction with another person (except for having sex, and even that can be done completely divorced emotionally from the other person), so they can be done in isolation and alone. These are self-made choices designed to satisfy self, acted out by myself. Are you beginning to see the pattern? *This is what self-centeredness looks like and this is why it is at the root of addiction.*

This is what self-centeredness looks like and this is why it is at the root of addiction.

Everyone does this. It is part of human nature, part of the broken state in which we all exist. When we put SELF in the driver's seat, all we can do is somehow medicate the discomfort we are feeling through the use of a substance or a behavior. Again, this is NOT what we were created for – to become masters at medicating our own pain!

As long as we keep looking inward for the solution to the discomfort of the feelings generated through life, we are going to be miserable. God simply did not give us the power to alleviate the pain of spiritual discomfort on our own when He created us. This is why we slide towards bad habits, negative patterns and even addiction when we try to live self-powered, self-centered lives.

Every time we experience a spiritual force (more on this in a moment) that is greater than our capacity to withstand, we are presented with a choice: turn inward to ourselves and try to overcome it with our own strategies or turn to God. Like I said earlier, this is something that happens CONSTANTLY to us in life. It is part of the way God created the world. It is something God built into the system of life so that we are forced to constantly have to consider Him! God wants relationship with us so deeply! It is His greatest desire! Here is what the Bible says about God desiring to know us:

This is good, and pleases God our Savior, <u>who wants all people to be saved</u> and to come to a knowledge of the truth."

I Timothy 2:3-4

and...

"For God <u>so loved the world</u> that he gave His only begotten Son so that whosoever should believe in Him would not perish but have eternal life." John 3:16

God knew this world would constantly present us with spiritual circumstances and forces that are greater than us – especially death – the greatest negative spiritual force. This is why he sent His Son Jesus, to conquer death and to save us from it. But he also makes the power available to us in this life to overcome all of the other negative spiritual forces that are set against us. Forces like fear, worry, anxiety, jealousy, envy, anger, grief, disappointment, sadness, aloneness, shame. These are the forces that can overcome us and drive us towards things other than God. Remember the cycle of addiction? We feel powerful emotions of insignificance, incompetence and impotence – these are powered by anxiety, fear, sadness, shame and other spiritual forces. Experiencing these forces causes us to crave relief, our minds start working overtime to create a strategy for relief and then we finally move to acting out with a negative behavior, bad habit or substance until we finally experience the negative spiritual force called "guilt". Then the cycle starts all over again!

There is a purpose in this cycle. It is to constantly give us the opportunity to look for something outside of ourselves, outside of things within our reach that can make us feel better, the opportunity to find something much more powerful that offers LASTING satisfaction. I'm going to show you how to find that, so let's keep moving forward.

BREAK POINTS:

- *What does this section claim as the "root" of addiction?*
- *Write down the ways in which you think you have acted selfishly or in a self-centered manner in your journal.*

THE MISSING PIECE

That cycle of negative patterns, bad habits and addictions just feels awful, frustrating and confusing. The problem with most of these things we reach for to find relief is that they actually work to some degree which just adds to the confusion. Alcohol works every time in relieving anxiety or fear – liquid courage it's been called. The problem is that the relief is only temporal – it never lasts and so we are eventually sent right back around the merry-go-round and the cycle starts again.

Something is missing in the equation. It's like the whole thing *almost* works, right? So to explain exactly what's missing, I want to use a story from the Bible as an example. It's a familiar story you may have read or heard before and it's found in John 4. It's the story of the Samaritan woman at the well. You can read the story for yourself, but here's the overview.

Jesus comes to the well in the center of town at noon, the hottest point in the day. No one else is around because the rest of the town typically comes early or late when it's cooler to draw water. But a woman arrives at the same time that Jesus is there. She's coming to draw water by herself because she's too ashamed to come when the rest of the town comes to get water. You see, this woman has a reputation in the town. She's "that" woman – the one that sleeps around a lot. The one that the townspeople talk about behind her back. Her life is haunted by shame, so much so that she can't go out when the rest of the townspeople are around so she goes alone at the hottest part of the day...and runs into Jesus.

The woman has been married five times and she is now living with another man that is not her husband. She is caught in the cycle of addiction – finding an answer to her craving in other men and they all keep coming up empty. She, like many addicts, has become an outcast and now is forced to go out to draw water alone where she won't have to be humiliated by the other townspeople. She is opposed and held in bondage by the powerful spiritual forces of guilt and shame and continues to seek relief through relationships with men. Jesus wants to rescue her from this awful negative pattern she is caught in.

He asks her to give him a drink. There is some back and forth between them which has to do with the local religious customs which says a man *shouldn't even be speaking* to a woman or be in her presence alone. (This is a fascinating exchange between them and there is a lot of rich material here worth digging into). Jesus couldn't care less about the traditions. He was interested in helping this outcast. Basically, the woman is surprised that Jesus would even ask her to give him a drink, surprised that he would dare to cross the cultural and religious boundaries...especially for a woman of her reputation. She asks him why he would ask her for a drink. Here's his reply:

Jesus answered, "Everyone who drinks this water will be thirsty again, but whoever drinks the water I give them will never thirst. Indeed, the water I give them will become in them a spring of water welling up to eternal life." John 4:13-14

You'll need to read the story to find out what happened and how the woman responded, but here's the point I want to make. God wants to rescue us from patterns and behaviors that hold us captive. He wants to give us the freedom of an abundant life, to break the chains of bad habits or addictions. He wants to replace our constant turning, to whatever it is we reach for when we are looking for relief, WITH HIMSELF.

God wants to replace our constant turning, to whatever it is we reach for when we are looking for relief, WITH HIMSELF.

God IS the missing piece. A RIGHT relationship with Him BREAKS every chain, every negative pattern, every bad habit, every addiction. God IS the fuel we were designed to live from.

This might not be news to you. Maybe you already HAVE a relationship with God but *you're still struggling.* That's OK. I did that too! I want to walk you into the thing that will make all the difference and take you to the place where you won't be thirsty anymore. You won't have to reach for a negative behavior, a drug, food, sex, porn, alcohol. You'll reach for the living water Jesus gave to the woman at the well and you'll never thirst again. I am speaking from experience. For almost 30 years, I was addicted to alcohol, pornography, sex, pills and I reached for anything and everything to satisfy the deep cravings for relief and NONE of them worked until I learned HOW to do ONE THING different in my life. That's what I want to share with you next...the SECRET to breaking negative patterns, bad habits and addictions.

BREAK POINTS:

- ***Read the entire exchange between Jesus and the woman at the well in John 4.***

- *What strategy did the woman at the well use to present a false self?*
- *Can you name the chief spiritual force working against the woman? What was she doing to try and medicate the discomfort of those forces?*

PART THREE – "HOW?"

BREAK IT NOW AND LIVE IN FREEDOM

I personally have spun through the addictive cycle most of my life, in spite of having a relationship with God ever since I was 17. So what happened? Why didn't God "work" all those years for me? Why would God allow me to suffer with something else controlling me for so long? Why would so many prayers for rescue go unanswered?

I could not have given you the answer I'm about to give while I was in the midst of my addictions. It took the clarity of real recovery to be able to say this, but here's why:

I REFUSED.

Yes, in my mind *I wanted* to stop doing what I was doing. *I wanted* to quit getting hammered on the weekends, feeling like I needed a drink EVERY night when I got home from work, secretly popping the pills, viewing porn, seeking out sexual satisfaction outside of my marriage, but at the deepest level of my heart, *I stubbornly refused to do the one thing God was asking me to do all along* – TALK TO SOMEONE about what was going on. I was so bound up by shame, guilt and fear that there was simply no way I could let anyone else in the world REALLY know the kind of life I was living secretly. There were things I had simply vowed I would never tell ANYONE – things I was committed to taking to the grave. *(You can read more about my personal story of recovery, rescue and redemption from years of addiction to alcohol, pills, pornography* and sex in my book "Broken to Bulletproof" available at my website **http://www.brokentobulletproof.com**).

For years, and I mean since I was a teenager, I had gone to church regularly, listened to sermons intently, been in Bible studies, men's groups, couples groups, gone to retreats, led worship and pursued God in every way I knew how…yet I still silently, secretly struggled with addiction and DIDN'T TALK TO ANYONE ABOUT IT! I clung to this verse in particular from *I John 1:9 "If we confess our sins, he is faithful and just and will forgive us our sins and purify us from all unrighteousness."* So, that's all I need to do – confess my sins to God and I'll be alright, right?

Kind of.

I had to find out the hard way what that verse REALLY means. It means exactly what it says – we will be forgiven and purified from unrighteousness. If we are in Christ, in God's eyes, he doesn't see our sinfulness when he looks at us. We've been forgiven at a spiritual level for all of the unrighteous things we've ever done and ever will do. But we're not *healed*. There is another verse that tells us how to be healed and it's in *James 5:16…*

"Therefore confess your sins to each other and pray for each other so that you may be healed. The prayer of a righteous person is powerful and effective." - James 5:16

This is where I was REFUSING. I REFUSED to tell anyone else about my sin. I REFUSED to allow God to work the way HE has chosen to work (remember, He's God, I'm not so He gets to decide this) which is *through TRANSPARENCY with other people IN COMMUNITY. These two things are the SECRET to breaking the bondage of negative patterns, bad habits and addiction.*

TRANSPARENCY and COMMUNITY are the SECRET to breaking the bondage of negative patterns, bad habits and addiction.

EVERYTHING changed when I did ONE THING DIFFERENT. This was the missing piece I needed to get well. A huge part of me changed almost overnight and then I went through a process of learning how to simply live differently, better, fulfilled, at peace, with purpose, in transparency with others in community. What the heck took me so long?

Before I figured out the missing piece of TRANSPARENCY, I had attended a conference to help me with my pornography addiction. At this conference, I remember them showing this video from YouTube that left an indelible impression on me. It was raw footage of a wildlife encounter from an African safari. A group of people are on one side of a river watching a heard of water buffalo move upstream along the bank of the river. What the buffalo don't see are three lions lying in wait in the tall grass and the herd is moving right towards them.

You can tell by the footage that the buffalo sense something is wrong even though they don't see the lions. They stop and appear agitated just before the lions attack. The lions spring forth, the herd turns and retreats madly. A small buffalo calf separates from the herd and goes it alone - it is singled out as the target. One of the lions takes down the calf in a violent tackle that lands them both in the river. The herd runs away in fear and disappears out of camera view. The other two lions join in at the river bank to finish the job on the calf and begin pulling it up out of the water onto the bank. This small, helpless water buffalo is about to become lunch for three hungry African lions. But the story is far from over.

Suddenly, there's a commotion in the water and the calf is suddenly being pulled back into the river! Now a hungry crocodile has joined the fray and is attempting to steal the lion's catch! An amazing struggle ensues – an intense battle for the next meal and the helpless calf is caught in the middle. But the climax of the story is still yet to occur.

On the far left of the camera's frame, the herd begins to return into view. While the three lions and the croc are battling it out for the prize of the young calf on the river's edge, the herd has banded together and is coming back to settle the score. A massive group of what appears to be thirty or forty adult water buffalo march steadily towards the fray at the bank. At some point, the lions and the crocodile all realize they are no match for the power of the collective herd of angry water buffalo. A scuffle occurs, the calf is released and the predators all scurry away for their own lives. The calf rejoins the herd, scarred and banged up for sure, but alive and safe within its protective family once again. You can see the whole amazing struggle for yourself on our website at *www.brokentobulletproof.com/community* .

This is a sobering, real-life picture of the power of community. Strength comes in numbers and isolation is truly a dangerous place which leaves one vulnerable. I want to share with you what REAL community looks like, how easy it is to find and how powerful is the force of healing that it brings.

BREAK POINTS:

- *Do you have a group of friends that will band together to rescue you when you are in trouble? If so, write their names down in your journal and say a prayer to thank God for them.*
- *Can you think of an experience when one or more of your friends came to your rescue when you were truly in need? Write that experience in your journal also.*

THE POWER OF COMMUNITY

"A new command I give you: Love one another. As I have loved you, so you must love one another. By this everyone will know that you are my disciples, if you love one another."

- John 13:34-35

"Empathy drives connection."
- Brene' Brown, Shame Researcher, PhD

Sitting alone in a hotel room with a bottle of vodka and bad movies on the TV is NOT LIFE. The vodka numbs. The TV distracts. The bed provides a place to be horizontal. The light switch in the off position provides darkness. Beyond the blood pumping through my veins, thoughts of despair meandering through my mind, there wasn't much life going on in that room. This IS the pre-cursor to DEATH and I have experienced it firsthand.

The primary goal of shame is to achieve ISOLATION. Isolation is the *opposite* of community. Best-selling author and shame researcher Brene' Brown, whom I've quoted earlier, defines shame as "the fear of disconnection". We experience shame when we are afraid that if others really knew us they would reject us. Shame drives disconnection from others and has a goal of bringing us to a point of total isolation.

Think shame isn't a big deal? I recently read an article about a man that was a pastor and a teacher at a Christian College. He was married for over 30 years and had two beautiful adult children. His family loved him dearly and he was respected by his colleagues and students. He committed suicide when it became public knowledge that his name was exposed on the Ashley Madison account list. Shame was the destructive force behind this man's suicide. *(read more at **http://www.christianpost.com/news/beloved-pastor-and-seminary-professor-commits-suicide-after-being-exposed-in-ashley-madison-hack-144920**).*

For so many people that struggle with negative patterns, bad habits and addictions, shame is overwhelming. So are the other powerful forces we've talked about earlier - fear, worry, grief, discontentment, resentment and others like these. When these forces become unbearable, it is almost a reflexive reaction to reach for something to numb us out from the emotional and spiritual discomfort of shame. That's what these negative patterns, bad habits and addictions are – OUR custom made solutions to alleviate the pain. The problem with numbing these forces is that you can't selectively numb JUST the specific cause of the pain. When we numb shame or fear or any other negative spiritual force - we numb EVERYTHING, including all of the positive spiritual and emotional forces in our lives. Good and worthwhile forces like joy, peace, contentment, clarity, motivation, trust, understanding, faith, hope and love are the forces of LIFE and they all get washed away in our attempts to numb a lesser force like shame or fear when we choose an addiction or negative behavior over a relationship with God, our Creator.

When we numb shame or fear or any other negative spiritual force - we numb EVERYTHING...

Here's what the Bible says about fear:

"For God didn't give us a spirit of fear, but of love, power and self-control."

-2 Timothy 1:7

Here's what it says about shame:

"No one who hopes in you will ever be put to shame..."

-Proverbs 25:3

These forces don't come from God...but the forces of LIFE DO. Here's what the Bible says about the positive spiritual forces of life - they are FRUIT of God's Holy Spirit:

"For the fruit of the Spirit is love, joy, peace, patience, kindness, goodness, gentleness, faithfulness and self-control."

- Galatians 5:22,23

When my own personal strategies to numb the pain of shame and fear FAILED me and landed me in jail, I was escorted into a new life and it started with one of my very best friends. I hit rock bottom, got arrested and spent a night in jail and when I got out the next day, I was thinking, "I'm going to walk to the nearest pay phone, hopefully stop by a liquor store on the way and buy something else to drink, call a cab and get a ride back to my truck," so I could be off and running on the wonderful strategy of life I had all planned out for myself. That would be the same strategy that had already landed me in jail - the strategy of "do what I want, when I want, the way I want." Great strategy. Instead, when I walked out of jail something unexpected happened.

My wonderful friend Mike was waiting for me in the lobby.

He had been waiting there for me for over two hours. I collapsed into his arms and broke into tears. You know what he did for me? He didn't lecture me or shame me for what I had done. He showed LOVE to me. He showed EMPATHY. He took me to get some food, told me it was time to get some help and drove me to another friend's house who let me spend the night with him (I was not welcome at my own home with my wife and family). These two guys started me off on a life-changing journey of recovery. As a matter of fact, if it had not been for them, you likely wouldn't be reading these words right now. *This is the power of COMMUNITY.*

Community is simply the formed circles of trusted relationships. It is a group (or groups) of people that care for each other the way they would like to be cared for themselves. People in community create a safe place for each other to be vulnerable. There is no shame in real community because the antidote to shame is transparency, vulnerability. My two friends Mike and Kent that helped me that day are two guys that I am "in community" with. We have lunch together sometimes. We go to church together. We meet in men's groups together. Our kids go to school together. We talk on the phone. We text. We hang out. We pray with and for each other. We each trust the others with any and all personal details of our lives. Both of these guys know EVERYTHING about my personal life because I trust them with it. They know details about my finances, my health, my sex life, my desires, my fears, my work, my marriage, my kids. They have allowed me to be completely vulnerable about all of these things with them...and they with me.

But Kent and Mike are part of just *one* circle of community in my life. There are other circles that intersect through having common relationships. My main source of community is a group of men that I meet with every Friday morning. We call it the Bulletproof Glass meeting. It's a place where everyone can be completely vulnerable and transparent. Sometimes we study a book together or a section of the Bible. Most of the time we just meet and talk, check in with each other, encourage each other, pray for each other. No topic is off limits at this meeting. Sometimes the conversation gets extremely tough, graphic, painful. Emotions flow in this meeting and I mean ALL kinds of emotions - sadness, anger, frustration, joy, peace. We laugh, we cry, we yell, we call each other out on our BS, we curse, we whisper, we pray. The only rule in this meeting is BE REAL...and everyone is. It is the most amazing group of men I have ever had the privilege of knowing. These are my "Bulletproof Brothers." My friend Mike is a key part of this group also.

I have another circle of community at my church. My wife and kids and I attend regularly together. But we don't *just* go to church to listen to the sermon and sing songs – yes, we do that. But more importantly, *we go there to help other people*. My wife and I counsel others that are struggling with addiction or a difficult marriage or relationship or finances. We don't have all the answers, but we want to give back some of what was given to us: GRACE. God has given us a unique experience which has equipped us in a unique way to help others that struggle like we have. In our church community, we have relationships with lots of other people we work alongside of there as well as pastors and staff members who help keep us accountable. Helping others at church counteracts selfishness and self-centeredness in our own lives and helps me stay sober in every way.

I also attend recovery meetings during the week. I'll typically go one to three times a week, sometimes more. In the beginning when I was struggling to break my addictions, I went daily because I NEEDED to go to stay sober. Now, I go to help other people. I go to welcome new-comers that are in the fight of their lives against their habits and addictions. My personal experience in overcoming my own addictions puts me in a unique position to relate to these people as well, which makes them willing to receive help from someone like me. I try to continually "sponsor" two or three people at a time, which simply means that I act as a mentor of sorts and spend time with them to walk them through the 12 steps of recovery. I am always a quick phone call or text away when one of them gets in a bind - to listen, offer an empathetic response, give advice if I can and encourage.

These are several circles of community that are all different but have one main thing in common – they are all SAFE places. What I mean by that is that they are places where I can be honest with others about what is really going on in my life and the people there are willing to listen. They don't try to fix me and I don't try to fix them. We listen to each other, offer encouragement, support, maybe prayer, maybe resources and we'll do anything we can to help each other. This is what true community looks like and it is fertile ground for recovery, redemption and renewal of LIFE.

Don't misunderstand this idea of community though. Just BEING AROUND other people is not going to make you well. That requires the main ingredient of true community: TRANSPARENCY, which is what we'll discuss next.

BREAK POINTS:

- *Are you involved in a "community" group of any sort? If so, describe it in your journal - what you like and dislike about it.*
- *When you meet with those in your "community" circles, do you primarily attend in order to "receive" or do you go with the mindset of "helping" others? Write your thoughts about this in your journal.*

THE POWER OF TRANSPARENCY

We've learned that shame drives *disconnection* and that it has the goal of moving us into isolation, away from community, away from the possibility of intimacy with others. It's a spiritual force whose power can be overwhelming and is the source of much misery. We've all felt shame at one time or another. Fear works in tandem with shame, keeping us afraid of disconnecting from others, facing possible rejection. Shame and fear and other similar spiritual forces like anxiety, worry, confusion, grief, anger and resentment are at the CORE of negative patterns, bad habits and addictions. These forces can *only* be broken ONE WAY: through TRANSPARENCY.

Transparency is the antidote to shame.

Transparency is the *antidote* to shame, fear and most of these other powerful forces that drive addiction. Let me give you an example of how the cycle of addiction works WITH SHAME and then to compare, WITH TRANSPARENCY. I'm going to use the same example we've used before, nail biting.

Let's say I face an emotional trigger of an angry boss that screams at me when I walk in late due to a wreck on the freeway; something which was out of my control. Regardless of the validity of my tardiness, getting dressed down by the boss in earshot of others naturally brings up feelings, emotions of anger (I want to yell back at the boss), fear (I'm afraid he might fire me) and shame (I'm embarrassed that he chewed me out in front of the others and I want to hide). That's the FIRST phase of the cycle of addiction – an emotional TRIGGER.

The discomfort sets in and I start considering ways to make it stop. This is the CRAVING phase. It's when the self-talk starts and I say things to myself like, "I want to punch my boss in the nose. What a jerk!" or "I can't wait until this day is over" or "That sucked. I'm so embarrassed!" In the CRAVING phase we are ruminating, consciously or unconsciously, on how bad the event made us feel and fully experiencing the discomfort.

Then we move to the PRE-OCCUPATION stage and the mind starts working overtime on the negative self-talk and it kicks into high gear, consuming my thoughts. It becomes hard to focus on anything else because this event has got me pretty upset. This is when I may or may not actually think about acting out, but I'm definitely heading in that direction. Since nail biting involves the simple act of raising my hand to my mouth, it's easy to jump from PRE-OCCUPATION to ACTING OUT without even thinking about it. More serious addictions may involve some real consideration about actually performing the ACTING OUT ritual.

Before I know it, I have my fingers up to mouth and I'm chewing away at the nails. This is the ACTING OUT phase of the cycle. Again, a bad habit like nail biting can happen so fast, I might not even be aware of my actions until I draw blood, cause pain or happen to look at my nails later in the day.

That brings me to the GUILT/REMORSE phase. I see my bleeding fingernails, feel the tenderness when I touch something and I'm reminded how much I DON'T want to do that to myself, how embarrassing it is when other people see my nails like this and I feel the GUILT and REMORSE...which can start the cycle all over again. At this point, there is little or no thought of the emotional trigger, but only thought about the guilt of acting out.

Now let's look at the EXACT SAME SCENARIO, except in this example we're going to introduce the elements of TRANSPARENCY and COMMUNITY and I want you to see *how the cycle is broken.*

EMOTIONAL TRIGGER: Angry boss screams when I walk in late which brings up feelings and emotions of anger, fear and shame.

CRAVING: I start considering ways to make it stop and the self-talk begins.

PRE-OCCUPATION: Okay, let's pause here for a moment. This is the moment when we introduce transparency and community. Spiritual forces of shame, fear and anger require a different remedy than acting out to bring LASTING RELIEF. Instead of allowing my mind to kick into high gear in pre-occupation, I pick up the phone and call a trusted friend (community). This can be a spouse, a parent, a pastor or just a close friend that you trust and can be honest with. "I got stuck behind a wreck on the freeway and I was totally late. When I walked in, my boss ripped me a new one right in front of the rest of the team. *I feel totally embarrassed and pissed right now* (TRANSPARENCY)." That's it.

That is TRANSPARENCY, THE SECRET to breaking the cycle of addiction, bad habits and negative patterns. When I tell someone else HOW I'M FEELING about the event that triggered me emotionally, it's like opening the steam valve on the pressure cooker. I have called a friend, been REAL with them about what I'm feeling and hopefully received an empathetic and encouraging response (if I *don't*, I might need to reassess if this person is truly helpful in my recovery and if they aren't, I may need to make a change). The power behind the drive to act out – REGARDLESS of the behavior – is radically reduced if not totally eliminated.

Now, I realize I have drastically simplified the process in this example, so let me fill in some of the blanks and answer some questions. First, being IN COMMUNITY is critical. Having pre-determined the person or persons you are going to call when you recognize that you are in the CRAVING phase or slipping into the PRE-OCCUPATION phase is mandatory. You can't make the decision of who you are going to call in the heat of the emotional moments after you get triggered – you need to know BEFORE it happens. We'll talk more about what this kind of community looks like and how it works in the next section, but for now let's assume you have done what you need to do and are IN community. This means you know BEFOREHAND who you are going to call when you get in one of these emotional situations.

Next, making sure the people that you are IN COMMUNITY with are safe, trustworthy people that have your best interest in mind is also critical. It won't help you if you call someone you thought you could trust and all they are capable of giving you is more shame ("Well, it sounds like you should've left earlier so you weren't late, right?") or empty platitudes ("That sucks bro. How about that game last night?!!). You're looking for someone that will give you two things when you call them, regardless of the situation you're in:

1) **Empathy:** Empathy is when someone puts themselves in your shoes and considers how you are feeling and is

willing to work through it with you. "Man I bet that feels terrible. I know how I've felt when I've been chewed out in front of others like that. I'm sorry, brother. I know you would have been there on time if you could have." Empathy is when someone is willing to emotionally "enter in" to your situation. This takes someone that is committed to your well-being.

2) **Encouragement:** Literally, to "give courage". We need our friend to help us re-order our thinking and put things in proper perspective when we call in these situations. "Look, you're a valuable employee to that organization regardless of how your boss feels right now. Tell me about what you have in front of you today and let's focus on getting some things done and putting that behind you. This situation and these emotions are going to pass." Those kinds of statements are simple truths, but they can be difficult or impossible to come up with on your own when you're in the fog of the CRAVING or PRE-OCCUPATION phase.

I know there are probably some that read this and say, "I don't need other people to help me with my nail biting. That's stupid. I'll go it alone." I get it. I felt the same way. The problem is, we've been "going it alone" for a long time and it hasn't been working. Remember the lesson of the water buffalo. We might THINK we don't need others, but we do. Even the strongest water buffalo needs the help of one or two others when confronting a hungry African lion.

In the next section, I'm going to talk about creating the kind of community that can do this for you. I am living proof of this. Transparency and community were the missing pieces for me in overcoming lifelong bad habits like nail biting and late bill payments to serious addictions including alcoholism, prescription pill addiction, pornography and sex addictions and more. When you combine the power of TRANSPARENCY with the power of COMMUNITY, you have an unstoppable combination that is powerful enough to break any negative pattern, bad habit or addiction. Now let's take a look at what this kind of community looks like, why it works and how to create it.

BREAK POINTS:

- *Describe the last time you were in the addictive cycle. Write down the details of what you were FEELING and what you DID in each of the steps in the cycle in your journal.*
- *If one of your friends called YOU with a situation like this, do you think you are prepared to give them an empathetic and encouraging response?*

THE CORD OF THREE (OR SIX) STRANDS

The first step in a 12 Step program is to realize that we are *powerless* over our addiction (or negative pattern or bad habit). The reality is, if we could STOP doing what we've been doing on our own, we would have already done it, right? (Not to mention the fact that you wouldn't be reading this book!) So the first step in getting help is to acknowledge that we don't have the ability on our own to stop. We've been going it alone, solo – a single strand of twine that just isn't strong enough on its own to withstand the emotional and spiritual forces that come upon us through everyday life.

So what happens when we add a *second* and *third* strand to the equation?

WE GET STRONGER. Suddenly, we now have the power to withstand greater and greater forces.

> ***"Though one may be overpowered, two can defend themselves. A cord of three strands is not quickly broken." - Ecclesiastes 4:12***

And we'll be even stronger if we've added four, five, six or more strands as well. Here's the deal. We need something outside of ourselves. We need additional power that we don't possess on our own. There is only ONE source to get power outside of ourselves – a power that is GREATER than we are, a HIGHER power: GOD.

The SECOND step in a 12 Step program is this: *"Came to believe that only a power greater than ourselves could restore us to sanity."* So how does this "Higher Power" relate to the cord of three or six strands? These strands that will give you strength are the trusted friends, the safe relationships you create in the different circles of community we discussed earlier.

PRINCIPLE: "Trusted friendships are built in the context of REAL community."

It's possible to be "in community" and not have any REAL friends. I did this for a long time – *years* as a matter of fact. I was in men's groups and small groups and large groups and couples groups. I led groups, I attended groups, I participated in groups. It wasn't that there weren't any people in these groups that were trustworthy because there were. Many of my closest friends today were in these groups YEARS ago. The problem was that I WASN'T BEING REAL with them. I was attending and participating in these groups but I wasn't willing to be transparent, vulnerable with them about what was really going on in my life. I DEEMED these people as UNSAFE to share my true self with. That's why I stayed STUCK in my addictions for so long – many painful years. So not only is it imperative that we BE in community, we need to commit to being REAL with the others we are around and in turn make it safe for them to do the same with us. And here's a secret I'll share: When I commit to being real with others and act in the courage of transparency in front of them, others FOLLOW SUIT and do the same. It is truly a cause/effect situation.

Here's how this plays out in my life, so this is a real-world example. I have enough self-awareness now to know when I experience an EMOTIONAL TRIGGER and I'm starting to feel the emotions I associate with the CRAVING stage of the addiction cycle. I can't control the things that trigger me and cause these emotions to fire off. I CAN, however, tell when I'm starting to feel and think the way I know will lead to PRE-OCCUPATION and slide towards ACTING OUT. So as soon as I start recognizing these feelings (which usually means I just start feeling uncomfortable in my skin, agitated, maybe I start noticing a short attention span or short temperament), that's when I pick up my phone and text or call a couple of the guys in my group. I give them a brief rundown about *what I'm feeling* (look, I know that sounds a bit weird, especially for men, but FEELINGS are the sign posts to potentially dangerous spiritual and emotional situations). The guys in my group will typically listen, empathize and then encourage me to take good, healthy steps in dealing with whatever it is I'm feeling. They help to "wipe the fog off of the mirror" so I can see myself more clearly. Many times they'll text me back and tell me they are praying for me or sometimes, if they can tell I'm REALLY nutted-up, they'll call and even pray with me on the phone. I do the same back for them as well. This has been KEY to me BREAKING my negative patterns, bad habits and addictions.

Look, the Bible tells us to "clothe yourselves" with the Lord Jesus Christ" (Romans 13:14) and that Christ is "in you, the hope of glory" (Colossians 1:12). God is in ME and God is in the friends in my community circles. When I reach out to them in my own weakness, I am HUMBLING myself and reaching out to GOD in them. "God opposes the proud, but gives grace to the humble." (I Peter 5:5). God shows his grace to me when I reach out in complete, brutal transparency to my trusted friends and almost

ALWAYS speaks through them into my situation, rescuing me from the cycle of addiction.

Do you have someone right now, that if you were feeling anxious, ashamed or fearful, you could call them and tell them *how you're feeling* and they would pray for you and encourage you? If you DO, you should thank God for that person. They will be the FIRST person in your strand of three or six. If you don't have someone like this yet, I'm going to show you how to make that happen and why it is so powerful in the next section.

BREAK POINTS:

- *If you found yourself slipping into the addictive cycle, who is the first person that comes to mind for you that you could call? Write this person's name and phone number in your journal.*
- *Do you have other "trusted friendships" that you could count as part of your cord of three or six strands? If so, who are they? Write their names and phone numbers down in your journal.*

WHO'S GOT YOUR SIX?

"Watch your six" is military terminology for "watch your back", referring to the 6 o'clock position. If a friend has "got your six", that means he's got your back, he's watching out for you. These are the kinds of friends I'm talking about surrounding yourself with in community. I met recently with a friend of mine who is an MD specializing in addiction recovery. He told me his own personal story and shared his secret that absolutely changed his life. He called it simply "THE SIX". He chose six of his closest friends, guys he knew he could trust and that cared for him. He met with each of these friends individually and asked them to be an accountability partner for him. He made one promise to each of these men: that he would be COMPLETELY, BRUTALLY HONEST with each of them about the intimate details of his life. NOTHING was off limits. These guys had full permission to ask him ANYTHING and he promised to answer with brutal honesty. He committed to complete transparency. They could ask him about his marriage, his health, his finances, his sex life, his thought life, the way he spends his time - ANYTHING...and he committed to answer them honestly.

He assigned each friend to a specific day of the week and set up a reminder in the calendar of his phone to call or text the assigned friend EVERY day just to touch base or check in. Sometimes it's just a simple text, sometimes it's a quick phone call, sometimes it's a breakfast or lunch meeting or a few minutes together at a coffee shop. Regardless, he puts in the effort to contact one of these guys EVERY day. The seventh day was Sunday where he would typically connect with one of them or another trusted friend at church. Otherwise, Sunday was a wild card day and he would call any of them at random.

My friend told me that once in a while it just doesn't happen and he isn't militant about making sure he talks to one of them EVERY day. If he gets slammed at work and life circumstances just don't allow for a contact with one of his guys, that's OK. He doesn't beat himself up and they understand as well. But he DID say that his serious commitment to the program has been the single best thing he's ever done for his own personal health and life. He has experienced growth in his career, finances, his health, his marriage and his other personal relationships. Having a team of trusted friends to "watch his six" combined with a commitment to being "REAL" (brutally honest) with them has been the key component in his own emotional and spiritual health.

I've experienced something similar in my own recovery from addiction and bad habits. I meet every Tuesday and Friday at 6:00 a.m. with the guys in my own men's group. We operate in a similar fashion as well. When any one of us finds ourselves in a difficult situation that is generating feelings and emotions like fear, shame, guilt, anxiety, worry, confusion, frustration, etc. we pick up the phone and reach out to one another immediately. This group now consists of 12 to 14 men, all of whom struggle with their own unique bad habits, negative patterns or addictions ranging from anxiety, struggles with finances, struggles with over-eating, pornography addiction, prescription pill addictions, alcoholism and more.

Here's the deal - when I'm feeling insignificant, incompetent or impotent and I find myself in the cycle of addiction, I NEED HELP

FROM A POWER GREATER THAN MYSELF. That's when I do TWO things:

1. **I reach UP**- God tells me that *"No temptation has overtaken you except what is common to mankind. And God is faithful; he will not let you be tempted beyond what you can bear. But when you are tempted, he will also provide a way out so that you can endure it." - I Corinthians 10:13* This is where I ask for help VERTICALLY, by praying UP to God. This action is symbolized by the vertical beam of the cross of Jesus.

2. **I reach OUT** - God is IN each of the guys that are watching my "SIX". By reaching out, being transparent and communicating what I'm feeling, I hear from God THROUGH my friend. He ALWAYS comes through for me in this way when I reach out. This action is symbolized by the horizontal beam of the cross of Jesus.

One night, I got a call from one of the guys in our group. His voice was elevated, tense. As best I can remember, the call went something like this...

Me: "What's going on bro? You OK?"

Friend: "Negative."

Me: "Where are you?"

Friend: "Out in front of the XYZ Motel."

Me: "That's not good. What happened?"

Friend: "I'm done man. I can't do this anymore. I am doing my best to get better (he was about a year sober from a porn addiction) but she (his wife) keeps rubbing it in my face. I'm so pissed right now I can't see straight!"

Me: "O.K. So what's your game plan? Why are you at the hotel? Are you really going to go spend the night in there away from your wife and family?"

Friend: "I haven't made up my mind yet. I was thinking about getting a six pack of beer before I decided. I figured a better idea was to call someone first."

Me: "I'm glad you did."

Friend: Silent for a moment. "Why's that?"

Me: "Cause I heard that hotel is notorious for bedbugs, bro."

He laughed. I asked him how he was feeling. He said he was feeling disrespected, angry, confused. We talked about those feelings and what was behind them – fear of losing his wife, his family, shame over his past addiction. I prayed against fear, shame, anger, confusion, pride. I asked for God's wisdom, clarity and peace for my friend. I reminded him that she had a right to feel hurt and betrayed and that he needed to take responsibility for his part in the argument because ultimately, his addiction had created the circumstance. He agreed. We made a game plan – he was going to drive around the block a couple of times, pray, bypass the liquor store and the hotel and then head home to listen to his wife. I had *empathy* for my friend in his situation and I *encouraged* my friend to do the right thing.

He called me the next morning to tell me everything worked out fine and told me thanks for helping him evade a bad case of the bed bugs. The thing is, we had had a similar conversation like this only a few weeks before and he was the one talking *me* out of doing something stupid when I was in the cycle of addiction myself and had reached out to him! This is just one example of how we take care of each other in the *Bulletproof Glass* community. We have ALL been on both ends of similar conversations with other guys in our group. These are truly life-saving conversations. We did not develop this kind of trust and understanding overnight. Most of us have been meeting together for several years and we've seen each other through some *wicked* trials; a night in jail, a divorce, the sexual assault of one of the guy's spouses, the death of family members, financial struggles, massive job changes, lawsuits and other legal challenges, broken hearts, broken lives. God has used each of us in different ways to minister to and carry each other through all of these things and more. Persevering *together* through trials like these have made our group *"Bulletproof Strong."*

Because we have all had the privilege knowing the intimate details of each other's lives, we have learned how to help each other in a powerful, effective way. This was not something we created, but this method really grew organically out of our mutual suffering and experience. It includes three key elements:

HONEST IN: We've learned how to be authentic with ourselves. We each have a heightened self-awareness of our own emotions, feelings, triggers, weaknesses. We are able to self-assess and name negative emotions like fear, anger, resentment, confusion, frustration, distraction, resignation, envy, jealousy, bitterness, pride, doubt, and a host of other emotions and spiritual forces. We can recognize when we are in the cycle of addiction and are able to take action to get out of it.

HONEST OUT: We've all learned how to turn to God FIRST before we reach for something to medicate or appease these emotions or spiritual forces and we do so by calling in reinforcements. We all will freely text or call individuals or multiple guys (group text messages) to *alert our friends that we have a problem and to ask for prayer.* Nothing is held back and we've developed brutal honesty, complete with graphic details and language if necessary, so that none of us have to carry a secret failure or rebellious sin.

HONEST UP: We pray directly to our Creator as soon as we become aware of a problem and we allow our friends to pray with us, over us and for us and our families AT ANY TIME OF THE DAY OR NIGHT.

Here's another REAL example of a text message string, and this kind of texting is pretty typical in our group. Guy 1 is a fireman and he works weird hours. Note the time of day:

> *Guy 1: "Guys sorry for the late hour. I am at work and can't sleep due to an intense headache and nausea and with that I am exhausted and I've been battling some triggers. I just wanted to reach out before any of this slips into preoccupation. Thanks I love you guys." 3:47 a.m.*
>
> *Guy 2: "Praying for you." 4:02 a.m.*
>
> *Guy 3: "Praying too man. Good job reaching out." 4:35 a.m.*
>
> *Guy 4: "Praying bro. Great job. Jesus be the answer to what (Guy 1) desires and needs now Lord. He is turning to you instead of the world. You are worthy. Sustain him now and remove his headache, nausea, anxiety and fear." 5:04 a.m.*

Guy 5: "Great job (Guy 1)." 5:43 a.m.

Guy 4: "Guys I could use some prayer also. Last night my wife was fearful, mistrustful and asked me if I ever had an Ashley Madison account because of everything she has seen in the news. I never did but just the line of questioning is painful, opening up old wounds for us both. On top of that, I'm getting ready to lead a recovery meeting this morning – major spiritual attack...especially with the big event coming next week. I'm in a good place spiritually but I know how fast it can go south so I would appreciate your prayers." 6:20 a.m.

Guy 5: "Praying now"

Guy 2: "Praying for you bro"

Guy 1: "I will be praying also (Guy 4). Thank you guys for the prayers. The Lord is good!"

Guy 3: "Praying for you (Guy 4). I can definitely relate as my wife has asked me the same thing out of fear and mistrust. I know how difficult that is and I'm praying God helps you work through it. I'll pray for your wife too. Also, I know you'll do great leading the meeting! I understand the anxiety though and I see it's a spiritual attack."

This is where miracles happen for us every day. We have learned, as a group, to reach IN and to reach OUT and to be HONEST IN, UP and OUT. God is ALWAYS faithful. We've learned that we cannot break these kinds of habits, patterns and addictions or grow to the deeper levels of our relationship with God ALONE. God created us for fellowship with each other and uses us in each other's lives to the extent that we'll allow him.

"Though one may be overpowered, two can defend themselves. A cord of three strands is not quickly broken."

– Ecclesiastes 4:12

"Iron sharpens iron, and one man sharpens another."

– Proverbs 27:17

BREAK POINTS:

- *How would you gauge your own ability to be "self-aware" (Honest In) and realize when you are slipping into the cycle of addiction? Use a letter grade from A to F.*
- *Grade yourself in a similar manner in your ability to be "Honest Out" and "Honest Up"- being able to talk about how you're feeling and what you're experiencing honestly with a trusted friend and with God. Write these grades in your journal.*

ACHIEVING PERFECTION (NOT)

Because the 12 Steps of Alcoholics Anonymous has been so instrumental in helping people break free from the serious addiction of alcoholism and changed SO many people's lives, including my own, I love referring to it as often as possible. Here is one of my favorite passages from the "Big Book" of Alcoholics Anonymous...

"Many of us exclaimed, "What an order! I can't go through with it." Do not be discouraged. No one among us has been able to maintain anything like perfect adherence to these principles. We are not saints. The point is that we are willing to grow along spiritual lines. The principles we have set down are guides to progress. **We claim spiritual progress rather than spiritual perfection.**"

- Alcoholics Anonymous, Page 60

We claim PROGRESS, NOT PERFECTION.

There is FREEDOM in that sentence. The goal of the principals of recovery in "BREAK IT NOW" are one and the same - to make spiritual PROGRESS and not to achieve PERFECTION. I work with A LOT of addicts and alcoholics that are in recovery. The VAST majority of us eventually have some sort of relapse or "slip-up" in their own journey of recovery - including myself. It's almost inevitable for most of us. Yes, there are the rare cases where people are able to get completely well almost immediately, but those cases are the *exception* and not the rule. Most likely, as you journey towards learning how to live differently and start experiencing freedom, you'll probably have a setback or two...or more. I have a friend I worked with for a long time that relapsed more times than I could count with alcohol, almost killing himself and ending up in the hospital multiple times due to his drinking – struggling with multiple relapses for over a year - and finally today he is living in freedom and now has well over a year of sobriety. There are MANY such cases.

My point is, don't get hung up on trying to be perfect in your recovery. *We claim progress, not perfection.* If you slip up and find yourself back in the pattern of addiction, that's OK - don't despair. There is ALWAYS still hope. You just need to execute your battle plan and get back on the horse. Here's an outline of what I call a "FIRE DRILL" - what you'll need to do if you suffer a relapse or "slip-up".

- **BE HONEST** with yourself and call it what it is - a relapse or a "slip-up" depending on the severity. Don't minimize what you did. Take responsibility for your actions and don't blame someone or something else for what happened.

- **ANALYZE** - what was going on immediately before and several hours preceding the actual relapse event? Were you feeling anxious, fearful, ashamed, confused, etc? If so, what was causing those feelings? Use this event as a learning opportunity to sharpen your self-awareness.

- **CALL SOMEONE** - call one of your "SIX" or another close trusted friend and discuss it frankly and honestly with them AS SOON AS POSSIBLE. Don't wait to be found out or "caught" somehow. Remember, the key to disempowering shame and addiction is TRANSPARENCY. Let them know exactly what happened and what you did.

- **RECOMMIT** - tell your friend you are recommitting to sobriety and make a commitment to call your friend DAILY if not multiple times per day over the next two weeks to a month to make sure you stay on track.

Look, none of us are perfect, so don't even TRY to be. Recovery and breaking these kinds of habits and patterns is about THE JOURNEY, not the destination. It is about SURRENDERING to God, our Higher Power, IN OUR BROKENNESS, not STRIVING to be perfect for Him. We are given one day at a time to live and this is how we must accept life now, walking through each day, being true to ourselves, others and God. THAT is the essence of "Esse quam videri" ("to be, rather than to appear") and the best way to live a life of freedom.

BREAK POINTS:

- *Write out a description of what "progress" will look like for you 30 days from now, 6 months from now and one year from now. How will your life be different, better?*
- *Write out your FIRE DRILL - what you'll do in the event of a relapse or a "slip up".*

STORIES

MIKE S. - Mike grew up in and around church and has had a solid relationship with God since he was a kid. He's married now and has six children and owns his own business. In spite of his rich Christian heritage and upbringing, Mike has struggled in his own life with bouts of addiction to pornography, but mostly with food. At the height of his addiction, his weight skyrocketed to over 310 lbs mainly due to his inability to control his eating. He admits readily that he struggles with eating for comfort, to medicate spiritual and emotional challenges.

Mike found freedom from his struggle with pornography and addiction to food through the principles in BREAK IT NOW and the 12 steps. He is active working with other men that have similar struggles and continues to live in freedom. Mike now weighs less than 235 lbs and is planning to climb Mt. Whitney this summer with some other men from his community group.

TIM M. - Tim struggled for years with a secret addiction to pornography which was having a negative impact on his career, emotional health, marriage and family. He also struggled with overeating and his weight ballooned to over 250 lbs. After finally coming clean to his wife about his addiction, Tim got serious about recovery and started using the principles outlined in BREAK IT NOW and by working the 12 steps. With the help of other men in his community group and by learning to live a life of transparency and authenticity, Tim has found freedom from his addiction and his entire life is improving. He now weighs less than 220 lbs. and he's also planning on climbing Mt. Whitney this summer with Mike.

Tim and his wife recently celebrated their 25th wedding anniversary, firmly on the other side of addiction, recovering together in a life of mutual trust and honesty. His career, marriage, family, health and friendships have grown in a way Tim never thought possible.

MARK H. - Mark is married and has a young daughter and son. He also struggled for years with a secret pornography addiction which progressed into an addiction to emotional affairs with other women. Mark knew he had to do something to break free from these addictions and started following the principles found in BREAK IT NOW. He's now been free from pornography and emotional affairs since 2012 and life is progressively improving in every way. Living a life of transparency has been the key to Mark being set free from the bondage of addiction.

Mark now works personally one-on-one with other men struggling like he did and is active in a community group of other men. He has a passion for being a positive force in the recovery of other men's lives.

DAN A. - Dan struggled for years with an overwhelming anxiety that held him bondage. He went through a difficult divorce to a wife that was an addict who wouldn't get clean herself. He is a single dad now raising his two sons alone. His struggle with anxiety has cost him in many ways, including damage to his family, friendships, finances, credit, health and career. Dan started finding freedom when he began following the principles outlined in BREAK IT NOW and decided to start living a life of authenticity and transparency.

Finally set free from anxiety, Dan just started a new job that is now paying him THREE TIMES his previous income. He also owns his own business which is flourishing, has paid off long-term debts which negatively affected his credit and is making plans to fulfill a lifetime dream of moving to Wyoming with his kids.

SCOTT S. - Scott was a classic example of appearing to be a man that had it all together with career success, a 30-year marriage, great kids, big house, he was a leader in his church, and he appeared to be in control of his life. But it was all nothing more than a facade to cover the brokenness and shame that spanned a 40-year struggle with addiction to work, pornography, arrogance, and later in life, alcohol.

Scott says that he spent years on his knees praying for change as he did not like who he was. Then the day came when he was revealed and he found himself at the point where he knew a change had to be made. He put all the chips in the middle of the table, sought help, and started a lifelong commitment to follow the principles that are outlined in BREAK IT NOW.

Today he is not controlled by addictions and he is looking forward to being married *another* 30 years with no secrets. God has also chosen to put two foster children in the lives of Scott and his wife, which they intend to adopt. In Scott's own words, "There is no way

I could have done this before if I had not made a change to a life of transparency and living the principles outlined in this book. I am blessed!"

THE ACTION PLAN

OK, so we've covered ALOT of ground and I've given you the foundational building blocks to overcome, recover from and break really almost ANY addiction, bad habit or negative pattern that you are held in bondage by. The only thing left to do is to create your ACTION PLAN and then EXECUTE IT!

Below are **SEVEN KEY STEPS** you'll need to take to get started on your own journey to recovery, BREAK the bondage you are in and move towards freedom:

1. **WRITE OUT SPECIFICALLY THE SUBSTANCE(S) OR BEHAVIORS YOU ARE BREAKING FREE FROM**

2. **WRITE OUT AT LEAST 20 NEGATIVE CONSEQUENCES YOU HAVE EXPERIENCED FROM THE USE OF THIS SUBSTANCE OR BY ACTING OUT THE BEHAVIOR**

3. **DOWNLOAD A "SOBRIETY" APP FOR YOUR SMARTPHONE AND SET IT TO START ON YOUR SOBRIETY DATE (see our RESOURCE section for some great recommended apps)**

4. **DETERMINE YOUR TEAM OF "SIX" AND MEET WITH EACH ONE (PREFERABLY IN PERSON, BY PHONE IF THAT ISN'T FEASIBLE).**

5. **SCHEDULE EACH FRIEND FOR A DIFFERENT DAY OF THE WEEK ON YOUR CALENDAR**

6. **SEEK OUT AND JOIN ONE OR MORE LOCAL COMMUNITY GROUP OF SOME SORT AND COMMIT TO MEET AT LEAST WEEKLY IF NOT MORE:**

    - *Your church*
    - *Alcoholics Anonymous*
    - *Narcotics Anonymous*
    - *Cocaine Anonymous*
    - *Gamblers Anonymous*
    - *Celebrate Recovery (great for almost ANY addiction or bad habit)*
    - *A Recovery Group at your church or synagogue*
    - *Start Your OWN Recovery Group*

7. **START LIVING IN FREEDOM BY BEING TRANSPARENT WITH YOUR "SIX" <u>DAILY</u> AND ACTIVE IN YOUR NEW COMMUNITY CIRCLES**

Look, this is where the rubber meets the road. But if you do these steps IN ORDER, you'll be well on your way to breaking free. Getting a solid group of trustworthy friends around you, being transparent with them about what you're struggling with and inviting them into the process of your recovery is LIBERATING and EMPOWERING. When I took this important step myself, I found that MANY of my friends admitted having THEIR OWN addictions, bad habits or negative patterns that they wanted MY HELP with, so it was a PERFECT FIT! I wouldn't be surprised if the same thing happens to you!

GET GOING! TAKE RESPONSIBILITY FOR YOUR RECOVERY AND MAKE IT HAPPEN!

LIVING IN FREEDOM

My life used to be full of fear, anxiety, worry and strife. I rarely had what I now know as "serenity". Even when I wasn't acting out or putting some type of mind-altering substance in my body, my mind was spinning like a roulette wheel. I heard a man in one recovery meeting put it like this:

"My mind is like Jurassic Park. There's a giant T-Rex running around in there chasing me and he's telling me if I would just take a drink, he won't eat me!"

Well said. I could TOTALLY relate. It's like I said earlier, the root of addiction, bad habits and negative patterns lies in HOW WE THINK ABOUT OURSELVES and specifically in selfishness and self-centeredness. Having a plan to counteract these kinds of selfish thoughts by being transparent with others and in a community of safe, trusted friends is the best, most effective and proven way to bring freedom.

So what does it look like to live in freedom from bad habits, negative patterns and addictions? Well, for one thing, the negative consequences start fading. They don't ALL completely go away, but the ones that linger, their impact is greatly minimized and they aren't overwhelming. Personal relationships grow, friendships deepen, trust is restored and you begin to start valuing OTHERS as more important than yourself. You become more SELFLESS instead of being so damn SELFISH and SELF-CENTERED. Life just WORKS better when we are SELFLESS because this is how God designed us to live.

I remember leaving a situation many years ago when I was drunk and had acted out inappropriately one day and as I was driving away and the guilt was setting in, I thought to myself, "This is what you're life is going to be like until you die. You're NEVER going to be able to stop this." Man, that is DARK thinking. At the time, it seemed SO true.

Now, several years into recovery I can see that that kind of thinking was a total lie. My life is NOT like that anymore. I WAS able to stop doing those things, not by my own power, but by the power of my great God and with the help of my trusted friends. I do my part, my friends do their part and God does His part – it works MIRACULOUSLY if I will allow it to. My life is REALLY GOOD now. It's not perfect and it has its ups and downs – that's just how life is. I am still tempted, I have bad days when it seems like a six pack of beer or a couple of margaritas would really solve a lot of my problems, but the TRUTH is – it wouldn't. Thank God I don't have to live like that anymore.

Now, instead of being a selfish, self-centered, isolated man, I get to share my experience, strength and hope with others that struggle just like I did. I find AMAZING amounts of satisfaction and joy in seeing others get well, recover and BREAK FREE from the things holding them in bondage.

Here's the most important thing I've learned in my journey to recovery. I can't offer my life to anyone to be of help to them if I am consumed with HOLDING ONTO it for myself. And the way God has designed the world, I can't RECEIVE LIFE, unless I'm willing to give my own life away by helping others. Jesus is my example for this. When I forget what being selfless looks like, I look to Him and remember His words…

"I am the resurrection and the life."

"In order to gain your life, you must lose it."

"Greater love has no man than this; that he lay his life down for his friends."

That is the ULTIMATE act of selflessness…and that is EXACTLY what He did for me…and YOU.

Please be sure to check out the additional resources listed at the end of the book. I also want to invite you to join our online community of fellow strugglers by subscribing to my blog:

http://www.brokentobulletproof.com

I am praying for your success as you take steps towards freedom, no matter what your bad habit, negative pattern or addiction, so that you can BREAK IT NOW.

Blessings,

TD Wilcox
Southern California

RESOURCES

SUBSCRIBE TO THE AUTHOR'S BLOG:

www.brokentobulletproof.com

STORE:

http://www.brokentobulletproof.com/store

MORE RESOURCES:

Alcoholics Anonymous	www.aa.org
Narcotics Anonymous	www.na.org
Overeater's Anonymous	www.oa.org
Gamblers Anonymous	www.gamblersanonymous.org
Pills Anonymous	www.pillsanonymous.org
Celebrate Recovery	www.celebraterecovery.com

MOBILE APP SOLUTIONS:

https://play.google.com/store/apps/details?id=me.deanhuff.companion

https://play.google.com/store/apps/details?id=com.ibyteaps.thebigbookofaafree

https://play.google.com/store/apps/details?id=ru.topot.cleancounter

https://play.google.com/store/apps/details?id=com.mirandadevs.selfhelp

https://play.google.com/store/apps/details?id=com.leoncvlt.nomore

SOFTWARE SOLUTIONS:

XXX CHURCH/X-WATCH Pornography Accountability Software
    www.x3watch.com

Covenant Eyes Pornography Filtering Software
    www.covenanteyes.com

VIDEOS:

Brene' Brown - Listening to Shame
https://www.ted.com/talks/brene_brown_listening_to_shame

Brene' Brown – The Power of Vulnerability
https://www.ted.com/talks/brene_brown_on_vulnerability

Johann Hari – Everything You Know About Addiction is Wrong   *https://youtu.be/PY9DcIMGxMs*

The Battle of Kruger - Water Buffalo Herd vs Lion Pride
https://youtu.be/LU8DDYz68kM

THE AUTHOR

TD WILCOX is a Christ follower, husband, father, and friend…not to mention a seasoned entrepreneur, mentor, speaker and author. He is the owner and president of his own marketing firm, The Atomic Group *(www.theatomicgroup.com)* and the founder of Broken to Bulletproof, a ministry focused on helping men and women that struggle with negative patterns, bad habits and serious addictions. Wilcox has recovered from life-long addictions to alcohol, pills, sex and pornography and now spends his energy on helping others caught in the cycle of addiction and searching for a deeper relationship with God. Follow him online at… **www.brokentobulletproof.com**

He is also the author of several books:

> *Break It Now*
> *Broken to Bulletproof*
> *Honest In, Up & Out (coming soon!)*
> *Nails*
> *The Joseph Scroll (coming soon!)*

For booking information/speaking engagements:
The Atomic Group
a division of Atomic Media Works, Inc.
TD Wilcox
P.O. Box 8007
Redlands, CA 92375
866.928.6642
twilcox@atomicmediaworks.com

NOTES:

NOTES:

NOTES:

www.ingramcontent.com/pod-product-compliance
Lightning Source LLC
Chambersburg PA
CBHW060202050426
42446CB00013B/2955